Reach Yo...

LEO

Teresa Moorey

Dedication

For my grandmother, Philomena van Eyken
my uncle, Alois van Eyken
and my father, Bartholomew Phelan

ISBN 0 340 69713 X

First published 1998
Impression number 10   9   8   7   6   5   4   3   2   1
Year   2001   2000   1999   1998

Typeset by Transet Limited, Coventry, England.
Printed in Great Britain for Hodder & Stoughton Educational, a division of
Hodder Headline plc, 338 Euston Road, London NW1 3BH by Cox and Wyman,
Reading, Berks.

Contents

Introduction

A PERSPECTIVE OF ASTROLOGY

Interest in the mystery and significance of the heavens is perhaps as old as humanity. If we can cast our imaginations back, to a time when there were no street lamps, televisions or even books, if we can picture how it must have been to have nothing to do through the deep nights of winter other than to sit and weave stories by the fire at the cave mouth, then we can come close to sensing how important the great dome of stars must have seemed in ancient times.

We are prone to believe that we are wiser today, having progressed beyond old superstitions. We know that all stars are like our Sun – giant nuclear reactors. We know that the planets are lumps of rock reflecting sunlight, they are not gods or demons. But how wise are we in truth? Our growing accumulation of facts brings us no closer to discovering the real meaning behind life. It may well be that our cave-dwelling ancestors knew better than us the meaning of 'holism'. The study of astrology may be part of a journey towards a more holistic perception, taking us, as it does, through the fertile, and often uncharted realms of our own personality.

Until the seventeenth century astrology (which searches for the meaning of heavenly patterns) and astronomy (which seeks to clarify facts about the skies) were one, and it was the search for meanings, not facts that inspired the earliest investigations. Lunar phases have been found carved on bone and stone figures from as early as

15,000BCE (Before Common Era.) Astrology then evolved through the civilisations of Mesopotamia, Greece and others.

Through the 'dark ages' much astrological lore was preserved in Islamic countries, but in the fifteenth century astrology grew in popularity in the West. Queen Elizabeth I had her own personal astrologer, John Dee, and such fathers of modern astronomy as Kepler and Galileo served as court astrologers in Europe.

Astrology was taught at the University of Salamanca until 1776. What is rarely appreciated is that some of our greatest scientists, notably Newton and even Einstein, were led to their discoveries by intuition. Newton was a true mystic, and it was the search for meaning – the same motivation that inspired the Palaeolithic observer – that gave rise to some of our most brilliant advances. Indeed Newton is widely believed to have been an astrologer. The astronomer Halley, who discovered the famous comet, is reported to have criticised Newton for this, whereupon Sir Isaac replied 'I have studied it Sir, you have not!'

During the twentieth century astrology enjoyed a revival, and in 1948 The Faculty of Astrological Studies was founded, offering tuition of high quality and an examination system. The great psychologist Carl Jung was a supporter of astrology, and his work has expanded ideas about the mythic connections of the birth chart. Astrology is still eyed askance by many people, and there is no doubt that there is little purely scientific corroboration for astrology – the exception to this is the exhaustive statistical work undertaken by the Gauquelins. Michel Gauquelin was a French statistician whose research shows undeniable connection between professional prominence and the position of planets at birth. Now that the concept of a mechanical universe is being superseded, there is a greater chance that astrology and astronomy will reunite.

Anyone who consults a good astrologer comes away deeply impressed by the insight of the birth chart. Often it is possible to see very deeply into the personality and to be able to throw light on current dilemmas. It is noteworthy that even the most sceptical of people tend to know their Sun sign and the characteristics associated with it.

■ WHAT IS A BIRTH CHART?

Your birth chart is a map of the heavens drawn up for the time, date and place of your birth. An astrologer will prefer you to be as accurate as you can about the time of day, for that affects the sign rising on the eastern horizon. This 'rising sign' is very important to your personality. However, if you do not know your birth time a chart can still be compiled for you. There will be some details missing, but useful interpretations may still be made. It is far better for the astrologer to know that your birth time is in question than to operate from a position of false certainty. The birth chart for Madonna (page 4) is a simplified chart. Additional factors would be entered on the chart and considered by an astrologer, such as angles (aspects) between the planets, and the houses.

The birth chart shows each of the planets and the Moon in the astrological signs, and can be thought of as an 'energy map' of the different forces operating within the psyche. Thus the Sun sign (often called 'birth sign' or 'star sign') refers only to the position of the Sun. If the planets are in very different signs from the Sun sign, the interpretation will be greatly modified. Thus, if a person has Sun in Leo yet is somewhat introverted or quiet, this may be because the Moon was in reserved Capricorn when that person was born. Nonetheless, the Sun represents the light of consciousness, the integrating force, and most people recognise that they are typical of their Sun sign, although in some people it will be more noticeable than in

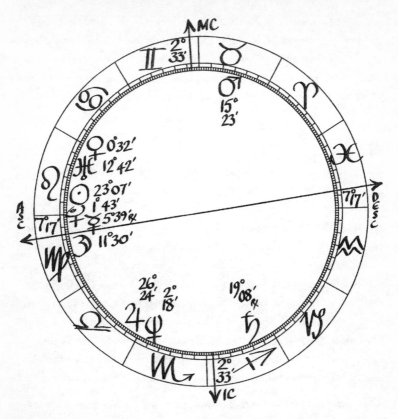

The birth chart of Madonna
Madonna is strongly Leonine, having Sun ☉, Venus ♀ and Uranus ♅ in Leo.
However, she has meticulous Virgo ♍ rising – which is interesting, for one of
her earlier hits was 'Like A Virgin'.

others. The planets Mercury and Venus are very close to the Sun and
often occupy the same sign, so intensifying the Sun-sign influence.

This book is written about your Sun sign, because the Sun sign
serves as an accessible starting point for those wishing to learn
about themselves through astrology. However, do not let your interest
stop there. If you find anything helpful in comments and advice
stemming from Sun sign alone, you will find your true birth chart

The **planets** are life principles, energy centres. To enable you to understand the birth chart, here are their glyphs:

Sun	☉	Jupiter	♃
Moon	☽	Saturn	♄
Mercury	☿	Uranus	♅
Venus	♀	Neptune	♆
Mars	♂	Pluto	♇ (♇)

Rising Sign or **Ascendant** (**ASC**) is the way we have of meeting the world, our outward persona. **Midheaven** (**MC**) refers to our image, aspirations, how we like to be seen.

The **signs** are modes of expression, ways of being. Here are their glyphs:

Aries	♈	Cancer	♋
Taurus	♉	Leo	♌
Gemini	♊	Virgo	♍
Libra	♎	Capricorn	♑
Scorpio	♏	Aquarius	♒
Sagittarius	♐	Pisces	♓

Using knowledge of the glyphs you can see that the Sun is in Taurus in our example birth chart (page 4).

even more revealing. The address of the Faculty of Astrological Studies appears in 'Further Reading and Resources' at the back of this book, and it is a good idea to approach them for a list of trained astrologers who can help you. Moon *phase* at birth (as distinct from Moon sign) is also very important. *The Moon and You for Beginners* (see 'Further Reading') explains this fascinating area clearly, and provides a simple chart for you to look up your Moon phase and learn what this means for your personality.

■ HOW DOES ASTROLOGY WORK?

We cannot explain astrology by the usual methods of cause and effect. In fact there are many things we cannot explain. No one can define exactly what life is. We do not know exactly what electricity is, but we know how to use it. Few of us have any idea how a television set works, but we know how to turn it on. Although we are not able to explain astrology we are still able to use it, as any capable astrologer will demonstrate.

Jung discovered something called 'synchronicity'. This he defined as 'an acausal connecting principle'. Simply, this means that some events have a meaningful connection *other than cause and effect*. The planets do not cause us to do things, but their movements are synchronistic with our lives. The old dictum 'as above, so below' applies here. It is a mystery. We can't explain it, but that doesn't mean we should refuse to believe in it. A little boy on a visit to the circus saw an elephant for the first time and said 'There's no such thing'. We may laugh at the little boy, but how many of us respond to things we do not understand in this way?

The planetary positions in your birth chart are synchronistic with the time of your birth, when you took on separate existence, and they are synchronistic with your individuality in this life. They have much to say about you.

■ MYTH AND PSYCHOLOGY

The planets are named after the old gods and goddesses of Rome, which in turn link in with Greek and other pantheons. The planets represent 'life principles' – forces that drive the personality, and as such they can be termed 'archetypal'. This means that they are basic ideas, universal within human society and are also relevant in terms of the forces that, in some inexplicable way, inhabit the corners of the universe and inform the Earth and all human institutions. Thus the assertive energy that is represented by Mars means energetic action of all sorts – explosions and fires, wars, fierce debates and personal anger. Put briefly, here are the meanings of the planets:

- Mercury – intellect and communication
- Venus – love, unifying, relating
- Mars – assertion, energy, fighting spirit
- Jupiter – expansion, confidence, optimism
- Saturn – limitation, discipline
- Uranus – rebellion, independence
- Neptune – power to seek the ideal, sense the unseen
- Pluto – power to transform and evolve

These principles are modified according to the astrological sign they inhabit; thus Venus in Pisces may be gently loving, dreamy and self-sacrificing, while Venus in Aries will be demanding and adventurous in relationships. Thus the planets in signs form a complex psychological framework – and that is only part of the story of chart interpretation!

In the old mythologies these 'energies' or 'archetypes' or 'gods' were involved in classical dramas. An example is the story of Saturn and Uranus. Uranus is the rejecting father of Saturn, who later castrates and murders his father – thus innovative people reject reactionaries, who then murder them, so the revolutionary part of the personality is continually 'killed off' by the restrictive part. The exact positions and angles between the planets will indicate how this and other myths may come to life. In addition, the mere placement of planets by sign – and, of course, especially the Sun sign, call forth various myths as illustrations. The ancient myths are good yarns, but they are also inspired and vivid dramatisations of what may be going on repeatedly within your personality and that of your nearest and dearest. Myths are used by many modern psychologists and therapists in a tradition that has grown since Jung. We shall be using mythic themes to illustrate internal dynamics in this book.

■ THE SIGNS OF THE ZODIAC

There are twelve signs, and each of these belongs to an Element – Earth, Fire, Air or Water, and a Quality – Cardinal, Fixed or Mutable. The Cardinal signs are more geared to action, the Fixed tend to remain stable and rooted, whereas the Mutable signs are adaptable, changeable.

SIGN	QUALITY	ELEMENT
Aries	Cardinal	Fire
Taurus	Fixed	Earth
Gemini	Mutable	Air
Cancer	Cardinal	Water
Leo	Fixed	Fire
Virgo	Mutable	Earth
Libra	Cardinal	Air
Scorpio	Fixed	Water
Sagittarius	Mutable	Fire
Capricorn	Cardinal	Earth
Aquarius	Fixed	Air
Pisces	Mutable	Water

Jung defined four functions of consciousness – four different ways of perceiving the world – 'thinking', 'feeling', 'sensation' and 'intuition'. Thinking is the logical, evaluative approach that works in terms of the mind. Feeling is also evaluative, but this time in relation to culture and family needs. This is not the same as emotion, although 'feeling' people often process emotions more smoothly than other types. Jung saw 'feeling' as rational, too. 'Sensation' refers to the 'here and now', the five physical senses, while 'intuition' relates to the possible, to visions and hunches. Jung taught that we tend to have one function uppermost in consciousness, another one or maybe two secondary and another repressed or 'inferior', although we all possess each of these functions to some degree.

Jungian ideas are being refined and expanded, and they are incorporated into modern methods of personality testing, as in the Myers-Briggs test. If a prospective employer has recently given you such a test, it was to establish your talents and potential for the job. However, the basic four-fold division is still extremely useful, and I find that it is often of great help in assisting clients to understand themselves, and their partners, in greater depth – for we are all apt to assume that everyone processes information and applies it in the same way as we do. But they don't! It is worthy of mention that the important categories of 'introverted' and 'extraverted' were also identified by Jung. In astrology, Fire and Air signs seem to be extraverted, generally speaking, and Earth and Water introverted – and this has been borne out by the statistical research of the astrologer, Jeff Mayo. However, this doesn't mean that all feeling and sensation people are introverted and all intuitives and thinkers extraverted – this is definitely not the case, and calls for more detailed examination of the chart (e.g. lots of Fire and Water may mean an extravert feeling type).

Very broadly speaking we may link the Fire signs to intuition, Water to feeling, Earth to sensation and Air to thinking. Often thinking and feeling are drawn together and sensation and intuition are attracted, because they are opposites. This probably happens because we all seek to become whole, but the process can be painful. The notion of the four functions, when understood, does help to throw light on some of the stumbling blocks we often encounter in relationships. However, some people just do not seem to fit. Also Fire doesn't always correspond to intuition, Water to feeling, etc. – it seems this is usually the case, but not all astrologers agree. Some link Fire with feeling, Water with intuition, and most agree that other chart factors are also important. As with all theories, this can be used to help, expand and clarify, not as a rigid system to impose definitions. We shall be learning more about these matters in relation to the Sun sign in the following pages.

■ THE PRECESSION OF THE EQUINOXES

One criticism often levelled at astrology is that 'the stars have moved' and so the old signs are invalid. There is some truth in this, and it is due to a phenomenon called 'The Precession of the Equinoxes'. The beginning of the sign Aries occurs when the Sun is overhead at the equator, moving northwards. This is called the Spring Equinox, for now day and night are equal all over the globe, and the first point of Aries is called the 'equinoctial point'. Because the Earth not only turns on its axis but 'rocks' on it (imagine a giant knitting needle driven through the poles – the Earth spins on this, but the head of the needle also slowly describes a circle in space) the 'equinoctial point' has moved against the background of stars. Thus, when the Sun is overhead at the equator, entering Aries, it is no longer at the start of the constellation of Aries, where it occurred when the signs were named, but is now in the constellation of Pisces. The 'equinoctial point' is moving backwards into Aquarius, hence the ideas of the dawning 'Aquarian age'.

So where does that leave astrology? Exactly in the same place, in actuality. For it all depends on how you think the constellations came to be named in the first place. Did our ancestors simply look up and see the shape of a Ram in the sky? Or did they – being much more intuitive and in tune with their surroundings than we are – feel sharply aware of the quality, the energies around at a certain time of the year, and *then* look skyward, translating what they sensed into a suitable starry symbol? This seems much more likely – and you have only to look at the star groups to see that it takes a fair bit of imagination to equate most of them with the figures they represent! The Precession of the Equinoxes does not affect astrological interpretation, for it is based upon observation and intuition, rather than 'animals in the sky'.

■ USING THIS BOOK

Reach Your Potential – Leo explores your Sun sign and what this means in terms of your personality; the emphasis is on self-exploration. All the way through, hints are given to help you to begin to understand yourself better, ask questions about yourself and use what you have to maximum effect. This book will show you how to use positive Leonine traits to your best advantage, and how to neutralise negative Leonine traits. Don't forget that by reading it you are consenting, however obliquely, to the notion that you are connected in strange and mysterious ways to the web of the cosmos. What happens within you is part of a meaningful pattern that you can explore and become conscious of, thereby acquiring greater influence on the course of your life. Let this encourage you to ask further questions.

Some famous Leos

Lucille Ball, Napoleon Bonaparte, Robert Burns, Cecil B. deMille, Alfred Hitchcock, Aldous Huxley, Carl Jung, Jacqueline Onassis, Mussolini, Princess Margaret Rose, Ogden Nash, Walter Scott, George Bernard Shaw, Mick Jagger, Percy Bysshe Shelley, Mae West, Rupert Brooke, Achille Claude Debussy, David Essex, Robert Redford, Coco Chanel, Zelda Fitzgerald, Beatrix Potter, Edith Nesbit, Emily Brontë, Madonna.

Naturally, all those in public life who have Leo marked in their charts will be able to draw upon the dramatic flair, charisma and strength of the sign. Leo's talents are equally at home in the arts, on stage or in any position of prominence.

Regal, Radiant or Tyrannical – what sort of Leo are you?

Here is a quiz to give an idea of how you are operating at the moment. Its tone is light hearted, but the intent is serious, and you may learn something about yourself. Don't think too hard about the answers, just pick the one that appeals to you most.

1. **You have been taken by a friend or colleague to a lecture on a subject in which you are, yourself, an expert – anything from flower arranging to brain surgery. After only a few minutes it becomes apparent that the speaker is waffling and seriously misleading the audience. Flowers will wilt or patients will be left with severe damage to the cerebral cortex, so you:**

   a) ☐ Stand up and challenge the speaker loudly and disruptively, to the point where you go up to the platform and take over.

   b) ☐ You challenge and make disapproving noises from time to time. At the end you stand up and roundly denounce the nonsense.

   c) ☐ You are aware that if you disrupt the meeting you will not get a true hearing. At the end of the meeting you take the speaker to task with a few dignified words. Then you seek out the chairperson and insist that you address the company at the next meeting.

2. **The PTA/golf club committee/board of directors is meeting to decide who should organise the school fête/Jack Nicklaus visit/ forthcoming merger.**

   a) ☐ Of course this should be you. If you aren't asked you will insist that you take charge.

b) ☐ As chairperson you will have influence over the proceedings anyway. Usually you are asked to take over.

c) ☐ No doubt they will come to you if they need you. It's of little concern to you. You have plenty of important matters to claim your attention.

3. **You have bought an outfit for a special occasion at a shop you regularly patronise (naturally designer labels and best quality). When you dress to go out you discover a fault in the material, right at the front, so you:**

a) ☐ Charge off to the shop and loudly demand not only your money back but some compensation for the inconvenience. It is outrageous to be palmed off with such inferior goods in a superior establishment. You won't shop there again.

b) ☐ You take the garment back and complain very loudly. The management scuttle to find a replacement and throw in a silk scarf for good measure.

c) ☐ You have plenty of eye-catching, high-quality garments. This is a nuisance. When you're next in town you take it back, of course, and obtain recompense.

4. **You once tore your jeans badly on a walk and went into the tennis club in ragged denim. You felt it looked attractively bohemian, and after all you can carry off most things. Then other people started wearing torn jeans and, lo and behold, they began to appear in the high street shops.**

a) ☐ You feel a mixture of satisfaction and disdain. People are always copying you.

b) ☐ You glow with pleasure. Yet again you find yourself in the position of leader and trendsetter.

c) ❑ You are deeply intrigued by what has happened and wonder about synchronicity and the collective mind. It shows how, when you are relaxed about yourself, you seem to be naturally part of the 'flow'.

5. **After that night of wine and starlight your lover has dumped you – can you believe it? – and is going out with spots-and-glasses from down the street. You feel:**

a) ❑ Outraged. You call your lover a fool, and tell him or her not to expect you to be waiting when it all goes wrong because you've got plenty more lined up. Inside you feel hollow, so you strut all the more.

b) ❑ Too proud to show your feelings, you go out with someone else. But you feel puzzled and deeply hurt for some while.

c) ❑ This must have some meaning in the course of your life and you ask yourself why. Your pride and feelings are deeply hurt – how can you use this experience to learn and grow?

6. **You are acting in the local Dramatic Society's production of *Julius Caesar*. Beneath your gown or toga you feel something snap and your underpants fall softly about your ankles. What do you do?**

a) ❑ This can't be happening. Managing to untangle one foot, and without forgetting your lines, you keep the offending underwear hooked about the remaining ankle until the end of the scene. Was that a giggle from the audience? Needless to say, next day the staff of the little boutique where you buy your underwear hear all about it.

b) ❑ Feeling the fatal sliding you know this has to be handled with panache. Calmly you step out of the pants, pick them up and fling them into the wings, continuing seamlessly with your lines. Later a friend from the audience asks 'Did what I think I saw *really* happen?'

c) ❑ You step out, pick up the offending undergarment and exclaim 'Gaulish elastic! Proof of the decadence of Caesar's Rome!' Then you stuff them up your sleeve and continue. Everyone laughs and claps.

7. **How you would describe your greatest ambition in life?**
   a) ❑ Money, status, power.
   b) ❑ Being looked up to, respected and loved.
   c) ❑ Self-respect, self-knowledge, inner conviction.

8. **At a party you are sounding off about your favourite subject when a newcomer challenges you about your facts. You react by:**
   a) ❑ Treating the intrusion with scorn, almost shouting down this rude person.
   b) ❑ You feel indignant. You give the impression of listening, but you want to discredit the newcomer and do your best to do so.
   c) ❑ Naturally you feel put out. However, these are facts you hadn't heard. You need to take them in so you can grow from the knowledge.

9. **At work reorganisation is in progress. Departments are being moved and work redistributed. How do you see your role?**
   a) ❑ You draw up an action plan and present it to the management – they could do with your help.
   b) ❑ You put yourself forward for a key position in the new organisation.
   c) ❑ You have enough to concern you. You fulfil your role with style, secure in the knowledge that you will receive recognition soon enough.

Now count up your score. What do you have most of – a's, b's or c's?

Mostly a's. You really can be a bit of a tyrant, can't you? Does it ever occur to you that while you are trying to rule the world you aren't earning much in the way of respect. Self-respect is probably somewhat lacking also, and perhaps your behaviour conceals some real insecurity. You don't have to shout so loud to be heard. Learn to trust in your true Leonine birthright. Hold your head high, keep your heart open and your mouth shut. You could come to appreciate that dignity achieves a lot more than bombast.

Mostly b's. You're a fairly typical Leo. You like the spotlight and you aren't backward in taking charge. Remember that the light that shines within is the light that truly counts – it is this glow that can light the dark corners when the applause of the crowd fails or wears thin.

Mostly c's. You're a fairly exceptional person, secure within yourself and shining with the light of true confidence and self-knowledge. This may intimidate people, and while you may say with some justification 'That's their problem', it does no harm to foster a little humility. You don't need me to tell you that you can always learn a little more, grow a little more.

If you found that in many cases none of the answers seemed anywhere near to fitting you, then it may be that you are an uncharacteristic Leo. This may be because there are factors in your astrological chart that frustrate the expression of your Sun sign or it may be because there is a preponderance of other signs, outweighing the Leo part. Whatever the case may be, your Sun-sign potential needs to be realised. Perhaps you will find something to help ring a few bells in the following pages.

1 The essential Leo

My mind to me a kingdom is

Edward Dyer

■ KING OF THE BEASTS

Sun-sign columns are usually excellent PR agents for Leo. Leos are warm hearted, impressive and charming. Endowed with personality-plus, they command centre stage wherever they appear. Playful, passionate and full of panache, they are everyone's dream date, and with their confidence and natural ability to envision on a grand scale they are the preferred candidate for any electoral constituency. It seems these sunny characters carry all before them.

There are certainly few of you Leos who do not blossom under the glow of applause, and many of you court it assiduously. Certainly yours is a regal sign, often dramatic and high profile. You are generally cheerful, hearty and not a little stylish. Even the more withdrawn Leos usually possess dignity and a quiet strength. However, with all that sunshine there are bound to be many shadows. We shall be looking at what hides in these and exploring Leo's true potential gifts, which are more akin to buried treasure than bright sunlight.

■ LEO BODY LANGUAGE

The defining word here is dignity. Although Leos can sometimes move swiftly, with the lithe grace of a cat, you are rarely hurried.

Your head is often held high and proud, and gestures may be sweeping, but seldom nervous. Leos do not readily display edgy mannerisms, such as nail-biting – you are continually and instinctively aware of the impression you are creating without usually giving the slightest hint of self-consciousness. Often you will quite naturally settle yourself in a position of prominence – out at the front or in a large, throne-like chair. You may spread legs or arms, taking up a lot of space without sacrificing one iota of grace. When you talk you do not like to be interrupted. Some Leos may speak loudly and raise their voices to drown out opposition. More likely they will simply continue, evenly and clearly, until the other person has shut up. However, many Leos are actually very unobtrusive. These people nonetheless have a certain 'presence'. Their eyes are usually fixed on a far horizon, even if the wall is only feet away and they give the impression of being preoccupied with something of great importance. Most Leos have an air of authority, but only a few are offensive with it, for they have the gift of a courtly charm.

■ MYTHS OF THE LION

The lion of the constellation Leo is usually taken to be the Nemean Lion, slain by the hero Heracles as part of his twelve labours. Heracles is in some ways a very Leonine figure. In the first place he has *twelve* labours, representing, some say, each of the twelve zodiacal signs through which the Sun travels yearly. Leo, as we shall see later, is ruled by the Sun. Heracles as a 'Sun hero' makes his way through his twelve labours, wearing the pelt of the first lion he slew, while employed as a cowherd.

Heracles

Greatest of the Greek heroes, Heracles was the son of Zeus and a mortal woman, Alcmene. Legend tells how, when he was a cowherd, two beautiful women approached him on the hillside. One promised him endless pleasure and comfort, the other great deeds. In truth the first was Vice and the second Virtue. Without hesitation Heracles chose the glory that comes from struggle and heroism – in other words Virtue. This was to characterise his life.

This is a choice that is central to many Leos and members of the sign can be found on either path. An individual Leo will not necessarily stick to one path – Leos are often capable of deeds that are noble, heroic and grand, but in smaller matters they may be indolent and selfish.

Heracles was born as the result of a prophecy by the titan Prometheus – he who stole the fire of the gods for mortal men and was punished for doing so by Zeus. Prometheus had foretold that the Immortals would one day suffer horrendous attack, and that the only way their opponents could be defeated was with the help of a mortal. Thus Heracles, by uniting god and man in his mighty person, represents something special and transcendent. He is both mortal and immortal.

For Leo this is an important point, for a Leonine life quest is to discover the goddess or god within. Surprisingly, that may only come from looking inwards, from times of heroic self-confrontation and honesty. The story of many heroes tells of trial, descent into some dark place and an eventual rebirth. This is a metaphor for the Leonine journey, for no Leo finds her or himself without tribulation of some sort that induces humility and self-honesty, so leading to a 'rebirth; in a broader vision that is not purely self-centred.

Before every Leo's head swells until it is too big for its name we need to consider some of the less desirable qualities of Heracles.

Heracles is stricken with madness and kills his three beloved sons. His wife Megara dies of a broken heart and Heracles, sanity returned, looks in horror at the devastation he has wrought. Now he must ask the Delphic oracle for guidance, thus his labours begin.

Heracles' madness and other tribulations are inflicted upon him by Hera, Queen of the Gods, because she is jealous of her husband's illegitimate children. However, in older legends the goddess holds supreme power, and Hera is really an ancient Moon/mother goddess, wielding the inexorable power of the seasons and of cyclicity. Heracles is an aspect, albeit disguised, of the Son/Sun god whom we shall be considering further later. He has no grave, being lifted straight from his funeral pyre into the heavens.

The story of Heracles hints that Leo, to obtain true glory, must make the 'hero's descent' from a position of comfort and supremacy into a form of surrender, into the chaos of the hidden mind, into experience of loss and unhappiness in order to discover her or his true strength and radiate real warmth. Indeed, this is a journey that we must all take at some point, but in Leo this is most graphic.

Finally, the lion is often referred to as the King of Beasts, but there are many, older Goddess connections. The lion or lioness is a 'showing forth' of the power of the Goddess. An ancient figure has been found of a lion-headed goddess in Mesopotamia. In Egypt the lion-headed goddess Sekhmet epitomised solar heat – Sekhmet has links with the most feminine process of menstruation, which we do not have room to explore here. (See *The Goddess – a beginner's guide* also published by Hodder & Stoughton.) Bast, the Egyptian cat-goddess, evinces gentler qualities of motherhood and protectiveness. The Goddess is often shown enthroned amid lions, and to this day the legs of thrones often end in claws, showing that the monarch derives power from the Goddess. Thus there are many feminine associations to be made with this 'heroic' sign.

♦ ELEMENT, QUALITY AND RULING PLANET

We have seen that each of the signs of the zodiac belongs to one of the Elements, Earth, Fire, Air or Water, and one of the Qualities, Cardinal, Fixed or Mutable. Leo is Fixed Fire. This means that while Leos are 'fiery' there is a steadfastness about them. Their sense of purpose does not leap and die but is more of a constant glow – thus they are less impulsive than the other Fire signs, Aries and Sagittarius, but they are more likely to finish what they start. Fire is a transformative Element of pure energy – it is almost as if Fire exists partly in another dimension, and this tells us something about Fire-sign people, in that they live in the world of the possible rather than the actual, they are vibrant with ideas, they inhabit the future – or perhaps the past – but rarely the present. Sometimes it seems they can see around corners. Fire people are enterprising and imaginative, and they envisage in a sweeping fashion – all these characteristics are strongly marked in Leo.

We have also seen that the element of Fire has some things in common with what Jung called the 'intuitive' function. This idea isn't quite the same as the 'gut feelings' of many Water or Earth signs, or the sort of message that Air signs may 'pick up on the ether'. Neither is there anything about it that we might term supernatural. Rather it is a perception of life that projects consciousness into the future and lives by inspiration and vision. This isn't at all airy-fairy. Leos can make the tea and do the shopping as well as anybody else, but inside something is probably going on that is anything but mundane. For Leo meanings and the larger framework are important, even if that tends to be somewhat repressed. This dull old world is not always kind to Fiery people. Leos may convince themselves that they are being purely practical, and they may feel they have to give that impression to others also. This happens despite the individualism of Leo, for the pragmatic is what is most generally respected in our culture. Deep inside, however, Leo is playing for much higher stakes.

Leo is the fifth sign of the zodiac. The astrological year begins with the surging energy of Aries, at the Spring Equinox. Then follows Earthy Taurus, sign of the Farmer, Airy Gemini, the great Communicator and Thinker, and Watery Cancer, sign of the Nurturer. Humankind has come forth to find its purpose, it has made connection with the land, thought and learnt to feel. One circle of the spiral is complete, and another begins with Leo, the second Fire sign. This is the sign of the Monarch, as if something has been achieved and Leo is saying 'This is what I am ruler over'. Hence the emphasis on consciousness, principally consciousness of the potential of the self, in Leo.

In the Northern Hemisphere the Sun enters Leo when it is usually the hottest part of the year, and yet Midsummer is a month in the past and now the power of the Sun begins to wane perceptibly, as the nights draw in earlier on sultry days. This hints at the regal nature of Leo, but also at the way this sign is called to look within, for temporal power inevitably dies. For those of you in the Southern Hemisphere Leo comes at the point in the year when light is beginning to grow, and yet vestiges of winter darkness still remain. We may rejoice in the return of the Sun, but we cannot yet forget the darkness that still lingers, and will return next year. Leo carries a message of the dark that hides in the light. This is evident in members of the sign, who find there are times when their light goes out and they crawl into a pit of their own making, or get in a gigantic bad mood when they speak to nobody. More subtly it connects to the 'inner journey' of which we have spoken.

Each sign is said to have a 'Ruling Planet'. This means that there is a planet that has a special affinity with the sign, whose energies are most at home when expressed in terms of that sign. Leo has for its ruler not a 'planet' but the Sun itself. The Sun lights our life, causing animals to thrive and plants to grow. 'Sunny' means cheerful, hearty, positive – everything depends on the warmth of the Sun. All the planets orbit the Sun, dwarfed by it and controlled by its immense gravity. To astrologers the Sun is 'leader of the orchestra' integrating the functions of all the other planets in the chart. The Sun gives the appearance of being all-powerful, and yet our lives also depend on complex and finely tuned Elements that have nothing to with the Sun. As well as life the Sun deals death, in deserts of searing heat where there is no water or shade. Here we have much that is relevant to Leo, whose power may be more apparent than real, who certainly has a negative side, and who needs to learn the lesson of responsible use of the influence he or she acquires.

◼ THE DIVINE RIGHT OF KINGS

In the late Middle Ages an idea evolved that was most useful to any crowned head – the power of the king came directly from God. Therefore there was no argument about any decree, what the king said was law, and not only temporal law. It was spiritual law, and to disobey meant that you paid the penalty, which was often dire, for challenging the Ultimate. This idea was one of the more preposterous heights of patriarchal totalitarianism and it was later challenged in the English Civil War, when the king lost his head, literally.

However, the Divine Right of Kings did not end there – not as far as Leo is concerned. For these people it is still alive and well, embodied in their own person! Yes, Leos can be quite insufferably superior and bossy. Sometimes condescending, egotistical and arrogant, they may behave as if they simply have the right. Leo is great at telling other people exactly how they should run their lives and expecting them to be grateful. Like an absolute monarch they can strike back hard if opposed.

You Leos are in no doubt of your importance. What matters to you is what centres upon you, and you usually believe that means the whole world and all the lesser creatures upon it. It is often hard to be sure how Leo has arrived at the characteristic position of prominence, for you are not often found in groups where the necessary skills are being taught. Far more usually you are up on the rostrum, doing the teaching. More than any other astrological sign Leos are proud of their birth right.

We have here an extreme picture, and by no means all Leos are rampant egoists. However, it is important to understand that Leos *need* to feel they are the centre of everything, they need to feel special, heroic, singled out for glory, because it is part of their life quest, and without it they are nothing. The world needs people who are prepared to be commanding, to stick out that royal neck, for the axe if necessary. Leadership, in the modern world, is becoming more and more suspect, and we prefer to think for ourselves, develop ourselves – which is, in itself, a very Leonine concept to some extent fostered by the passage of the planet Pluto through Leo in the late 1940s and early 1950s. However, the world needs beacons to follow, and someone with Leonine courage and conviction to raise them, even if, in the absence of Divine Right, there are few followers.

Leonine self-importance is quite necessary to the essential life purpose of the sign. Leo is on a quest for the self, the true self. Jung, himself a Leo, founder of analytical psychology and one of the finest and most imaginative minds of the twentieth century, defined the purpose of the human personality as the process of individuation. This is the process of becoming oneself, of bringing into consciousness that which is hidden, repressed or unavailable, of redeeming what is lost and of achieving a balance and completeness that is greater than the sum of its parts. The symbol of the individuated self is the mandala – any circular, balanced structure, such as the wheel of the zodiac itself. Individuation is quite hard to define, in essence, for it is a spiritual goal quite beyond ordinary 'self-development'. Naturally to achieve this you need to start, in part, from the perspective of yourself as central, and to concentrate upon yourself as upon a kingdom. In a sense, individuation is the highest form of power. It is a far cry from the old domineering and arrogant image, which is in fact a distortion of Leo's true purpose.

■ PURRING PUSSYCATS

Do these superior Leonine souls ever unbend a little? Most certainly they do. One thing that all the Fire signs love is play. They have a childlike core and a certain innocence. Instinctively they know that in play we lose ourselves to find ourselves. More than this, Leo has a huge capacity to enjoy life. There is something about playing that reconnects us to a simpler, more vivid part of ourselves that we may have left behind in childhood. In the case of Leo this isn't usually very far behind!

One delightful Leo friend of mine told me about a workshop she had attended on the subject 'Redeeming the Magical Child Within'. What a lovely Leonine metaphor, 'magical child' full of freshness, possibilities and requited creativity! In this workshop each participant was given a teddy bear and my friend spoke with delight about her lovely teddy and all this had meant to her in terms of rediscovering things about herself, her childhood and her capacity to enjoy. 'The only trouble was', she said, 'we all had to give our teddies back!'

If you are a Leo you don't necessarily need a teddy to find your magical child. Anything that allows you to play, that takes you away from the day to day, that connects you with a wider world of possibilities where your imagination can take flight – anything such will suffice, indeed it is deeply necessary. Seek it. Give yourself permission to enjoy. Leo should be given the opportunity to find this space. Just watch that big cat roll over on its back and purr!

■ LORD OF ALL I SURVEY

We haven't finished with Leo dogmatism and self-importance as yet. While we need to remind ourselves that it often arises from healthy impulses – and that by no means do all Leos exhibit these characteristics in the first place – nonetheless the King of the Beasts can get quite out of hand at times and then the law of the jungle operates. Leo's Law goes something like this 'I'm always right. Further than this, I'm always magnanimous. I'm wonderful and so everything good I see must have arisen from me, and that includes any bright ideas you may think you've had, and to challenge me means you are a small-minded fool.' The small print reads 'Don't *ever* accuse me of anything, least of all being petty or underhand'.

I saw this law in operation in a group I once attended as part of my training. The man who ran it was a warm-hearted Leo, who could nonetheless be highly objectionable, at times. In particular he was adept at ruffling the fur of all the younger males, whom he may have imagined were going to challenge him – but they didn't! As a regular gesture of magnanimity he would gather us together for an opportunity to express any criticisms we might have about the course. Warm smiles and an avuncular manner coaxed forth all the grievances, most of which were sensibly formulated. Then guess what? All our objections were gently, but insistently 'given back to us,' and we were admonished to work on ourselves. If we felt we had been pushed too hard, why then perhaps we had a problem with authority figures. Felt our wishes hadn't been heard? Perhaps this was a legacy of a parental figure whom we felt ignored us, thus we were currently unable to express our feelings coherently – and so it went on. Nothing anyone said ever dented this man's total assurance when it came to shaking anything and everything off his lordly back. At the end of such sessions he would wear a long-suffering smile and seemed oblivious to the seething emotions of all the lesser mortals. I must say, in his defence, that when someone finally found the courage to confront him with what he was doing (at the risk of being accused of closet patricide) he did have the grace to back down, saying 'You may have a point'. Long live the king!

Leos do sometimes have a way of steaming into people's lives, taking over and then making the benefactee feel very, very small if he or she raises the tiniest objection. Similarly, a Leo directing anything from a play to a multinational company may annexe the ideas of underlings as his or her own, and when confronted by this will have a response on the lines of 'How could you suggest such a thing – of *me*! After all I've done for you.' Really this almost amounts to emotional manipulation, for in such circumstances the burden of nameless guilt carried by most of us is activated. The outrage of Leo convinces others that they must have done *something* wrong! However, Leo isn't acting from an instinctive knowledge of human nature, but from an instinctive need to preserve supremacy. Such a Lion is a cowardly Lion. Others should pity Leo (they *hate* that!) be patient with them, mark their good points – and keep silent!

■ NEVER SAY DIE

We mentioned a dirty word, in the previous paragraph – cowardice. A secret of many Leos is that they deeply fear that they are really cowards – small people with little or nothing special about them. Like the lion in *The Wizard of Oz* they may spend much of their lives looking for their courage, and *en route* there may be much of the sort of posturing we have been considering. The truth of the matter is that this sign has all the trappings of what we might call true courage, and this does not surface until Leo faces a challenge – a sick spouse, a financial disaster. Meanwhile Leo is busy keeping up appearances. That means the Sun always shines – a scientific impossibility and a great personal strain. You need to learn to allow yourself to 'die', to go within, out of the light. Only in this way have you a hope of building something that is real and meaningful, something that is not just 'sound and fury'. By having the courage to fail, to accept defeat, to look inadequate, to examine yourself inside can you find a truly rich and rewarding existence.

The son / lover

Many ancient myths tell of the consort to the Goddess, who is born as Her son, grows to maturity, becomes Her lover, dies and is reborn as the son of His own fathering. No incest is implied – simply the Goddess is seen as the Mother of All while the God is the power of life that ebbs and flows. There are many goddess/god duos – Cybele and Attis from Anatolia, Aphrodite and Adonis from Greece, Isis and Osiris/Horus from Egypt, and so on. These stories arise from more ancient, matrifocal consciousness, where the Goddess is seen as the cycle – changing appearance perhaps (for many goddesses were linked with the Moon) but not essence. The God, on the other hand is He who travels the cycle, being born, maturing, dying and next year born again. Needless to say, the Sun is a representation of the God, dying in winter, reborn in spring.

There is a wisdom in this myth for it speaks of the necessity to die, to let go, to go within. Our culture has ignored this and we strive to build bastions of power, immutable structures from skyscrapers through scientific 'certainties' and religious dogmas. The dangers of this – global destruction, no less – are becoming appreciated. For Leo, sign of the Sun, the message is obvious. You can't always shine, nor is it right that you should. Winter comes – and the spring comes behind and all is infused with fresh vigour. Be prepared to 'die' to recede, to go within. Yours is a nature of tremendous breadth of vision, generosity and strength. Give yourself the chance to make contact with your deepest inner wells – there is your treasure.

■ PRACTICE AND CHANGE ■

● If you are a Leo it is natural to you to seek centre stage, and while in some Leos this is hardly in evidence, yet deep within you have the conviction that all revolves around you. In some ways it does. You don't need me to give you permission to shine. Remember, however, that your true power comes not from 'lording it' over people but from discovering you own essence – there lies your real brilliance.

● Are you afraid that you lack courage? Answer truthfully, where lie your fears? Are they moral, emotional, physical? Face them. Now you know that you do not lack courage, for courage is about facing fears, not denying them.

● Are you a Leo which is always playing to the gallery? That applause never really gets to where it matters, does it? You just need more and more 'fixes'. Learn to be your own appreciative audience.

● Never forget the importance of play. Enjoy yourself.

● Don't forget the importance of 'letting go'. You may find this hard; imagining sunset or midwinter may help. Be prepared to have times of quiet, where you have an opportunity to go within. Merely being on your own may not suffice, for we can still live up to expectations – our own, or others – even when we are solitary. Try to let go of goals, stereotypes and ambitions, and commune with yourself. You may find meditation helps.

● It is hard for you to learn humility, and no one is suggesting that you grovel – heaven forbid. However, from a certain humility comes true dignity and it wins respect – especially self-respect. You cannot be always right. Give other people their space, a hearing and some respect also.

2 Relationships

. . . She'is all States, and all Princes, I,
Nothing else is.
Princes doe but play us; compar'd to this;
All honor's mimique: All wealth alchimie.
Thou sunne art halfe as happ'as wee,
In that the world's contracted thus;
. . . Shine here to us, and thou art every where;
This bed thy center is, these walls thy spheare

John Donne, *The Sunne Rising*

Leos don't do many things by halves and your relationships are no exception. Leo in love is whole hearted, dramatic and passionate, and if a certain extra pathos can be injected, or even a mythical flavour, then so much the better. Not that you are drawn to tortured longings or a yearning for the forbidden – although this may happen on the odd occasion. Certainly you are greatly averse to anything sordid or hole in corner. Yet if the dramatic voltage can be stepped up a little, you shine all the brighter. The days of heroism are long past, but they linger in the heart of every Leo.

There are rarely half-measures when it comes to love for the sign of the Lion. Real feeling and commitment are high on the list of priorities, along with sexual gratification, true companionship and status. It is this final requirement that can get Leos into the most trouble of all, for their big hearts will heal, if they are broken (and it happens . . . it happens). However, a Lion in a cage formed by convention and material trappings is a savage and unhappy beast.

The urge for security is stronger in Leo than in the other Fire signs. You also do appreciate comfort (you appreciate splendour even more!) and you may be swayed by the promise of this and your own secret self-doubts, into an early marriage or committed partnership that has little hope of sustaining your ardour. Once promised, Leos do not like to renege or cheat and you may spend years deeply unhappy, lonely and frustrated before getting together the resolve to leave. You are not quitters. Mostly you are too honourable or indolent to have affairs – although occasionally a Leo with a rapacious vanity will gobble up as many sexual partners as possible, but that is rare. Leos take relationships seriously. You give a lot and you expect a lot in return, but you do need to be more cautious and thoughtful before giving heart and/or hand. There is an old song that goes 'Don't throw your love away . . . for you might need it some day.' This ought to be the anthem of romantic Leo.

■ LEONINE SEXUALITY

As with all the Fire signs, a fantasy element is very important for Leo when it comes to sex. The setting should be right, and that means the more opulent the better. Candlelight, soft music and satin sheets on a king-size bed set the scene ... I'm sure you get the picture. There should be always a hint of the special. After all, everyone can afford a candle, and for the instant transformation of the scruffy to the magical, candlelight is favourite. Add a bottle of good wine and some music, and the Lion may start to purr.

Of much greater importance, however, is the relationship itself, and again that should contain some fantasy. By this I certainly do not mean that the partners of Leo have to pretend to be secret agents or reincarnations of Cleopatra or El Cid. Again 'special' is the keyword. Over the first intimate dinner Leo does not want to hear about the blocked lavatory at the office or what a friend thinks is the best cure for acne. You Leos want to hear about your partner's dreams, about anything interesting that has happened, about anything that will make you laugh, and about what makes your partner unique – at your best you can make your partner feel special, too. Leos like to laugh, and any dreams your partner narrates should not totally exclude you, by implication. Above all, a partner should show you that he or she finds you fascinating, and is listening to every word – this is a great turn-on to the Lion, who may be secretly insecure. However, sycophants are definitely not on the menu. How can you value their good opinion if it is not evident that they are thinking for themselves?

Leo is a very passionate sign and desire runs high and constant. You are not easily diverted if you have decided someone is for you. However, again like the other Fire signs, your eyes are often too big for your belly (or other anatomical parts). Despite your strong feelings, Leos are not sexual marathon candidates, as may be Taurus or Scorpio, when in the mood. Life is just never the stuff of dreams and your Leonine big expectations tend to leave you deflated. This isn't always noticeable, for as we have said, there is much constancy in Leo. However, when anything is brought down to earth it contains that little kernel of disappointment. A Leo lover will continue to enthuse and secretly mythologise, if the truth were known. However, the nitty-gritty of daily life afflicts Leo with a vague sense of disenchantment. You Leos need to remember that the ideal or the transcendent can never be fully fleshed out, but that does not mean that transcendence is not available. It comes from within, and from the spirit. This certainly doesn't imply the need for celibacy – Leo doesn't take to that. However, it means turning away from the literal and learning to generate a sense of meaning yourself, on another level. More simply it means retaining your imagination and zest in the face of moods and wet Mondays and generating an extra 'something'. More Earthy people may see this as gibberish, but many Leos will find much here that makes sense.

Female Leo

Ms Leo is a highly sexed and responsive lady. Her ego is flattered (well – surprise, surprise!) at compliments and attention, and she is often pursued by a group of admirers. She's a great flirt, having perfected an art of languid posing and head-tossing that is equally at home in drawing room or jungle. It is more the law of the jungle that applies to rivals, however. The Lioness can show her claws if anyone approaches her man, or if any attractive female comes into too close an orbit. Leo ladies often choose rather plain companions rather than share the limelight. They love being wined and dined and treated like film stars and will rarely refuse an opportunity for this, if it is offered. However, if Ms Leo says 'yes' to a date it means just that – yes, she will go out with the man. If he spends a month's salary on entertaining her, well she's merely being treated as the queen she is. He definitely hasn't bought her sexually, and to assume this is to risk a sharp rebuke, or worse. Ms Leo isn't manipulating him or taking him for a mug, she's merely taking what he has apparently been happy to give to her royal self, for the pleasure of her company.

On the other hand, if the Lioness is in love – or something approaching it – she will be quite plainly 'hot stuff'. This certainly doesn't mean that her lover can treat her without respect or assume she will have sex on the first night. No, such matters require build up and atmosphere. When Ms Leo decides to give herself she does so with customary generosity and passion. If he fumbles with the contraceptives, he should turn it into a joke and never forget to keep making her feel she's the most desirable woman on Earth.

After all, she is, isn't she? He should make like the King of the Jungle for that's what he is, right now.

Male Leo

Mr Leo may be a slightly more complex soul. Yes, there is the passion and also the commitment, but it has to be said that Mr Leo's ego does give him a little trouble on occasion. It is rare for Mr Leo to turn into a bed-hopping Don Juan, for his need for intimacy and his natural indolence make this unsatisfactory and uncomfortable. However, some Leos do have a string of partners – not really because the partners don't match up to expectations – although Mr Leo may tell himself it's that. Rather it's because Mr Leo himself doesn't come up to his own rigorous standards, and a partner may be a reminder of what he sees as his own inadequacy, or what he would see as inadequacy if he dared to look it in the face. Horrors! Much better to prowl off in search of greater glory. Sooner or later this palls, however, and lonely Mr Leo is left with some solid self-confrontation if life and relationships are ever to shape up.

Most Leos, however, are wonderful lovers. They put a great deal into love-making – they do want the earth to move, and while they may think they are most concentrated on the physical, this isn't in fact the case. Mr Leo is proving something to himself, and to his lover. He is also wanting this to be a beautiful and deeply enjoyable experience. Because of this he isn't always on for an instant repeat performance. The Lion may be drained by his efforts, because they have involved heart and soul as well as body. Gentle massage of body and ego will help him recover, if that's what his lover wants. Most of all – and we can't repeat this enough – his lover should make him feel appreciated, special, even god-like. If she gets this right, she may well have him eating out of her hand – in a dignified way, of course!

The story of Icarus

Icarus's father was the noted craftsman, Daedalus, who devised the Cretan labyrinth, where dwelt the horrific Minotaur, bull-headed man who devoured human flesh. Because Daedalus revealed the secrets of the maze, King Minos of Crete imprisoned him and his son in a tower. However, the king had reckoned without the resourcefulness and skill of the craftsman, for Daedalus fashioned wings from feathers and wax, and strapping them to the arms of himself and his son he escaped from the tower on the winds of dawn.

Daedalus had warned Icarus that he must not fly too near the Sun, or the wax of the wings would melt and he would fall to his death. But Icarus, enchanted by the power of flight, forgot his advice. Full of his new skill, Icarus felt omnipotent, immortal. 'Hello, Lord Apollo,' he called, impudently, as he flew nearer and nearer to the flaming disk of the Sun. He did not notice the slow drip, drip of the wax as the great heat began to melt it. Soon he found he was losing altitude. All the wax was overheated. It liquified, the wings fell apart and Icarus plunged to his death.

This is a cautionary tale indeed, about inflated sense of self and general needlessness. For Leo it is a metaphor for what can occur if a sense of proportion is not maintained, and while this applies to all areas of life, it is particularly important in Leo's relationships. Leo must quite simply not expect too much, must not aspire to god-like heights, or the risk of disillusion and a dizzying fall is courted. Rather than becoming like Icarus, Leo needs to emulate Daedalus – clever enough to master flight, clever enough to know when to come in to land. In this way Leo brings just a little of the divine down on to the hard earth and provides a place in the Sun, both for self and companions.

■ LEO WOMAN IN LOVE

The man who has won the heart of Ms Leo may well be the envy of all his mates. Striking and sensuous, Ms Leo knows just how to cross those satin-clad legs to give a flash of black lace, and while she may regard it as her right to turn heads, her heart is usually given to one alone.

There can be a wild side to some Leo ladies but for preference they prefer one mate. Of course, there are also female Leos who are less noticeable, but these nonetheless usually exude an air of dignity and self-assurance, and have a subtle way of making one feel it is a privilege to be with them, let alone loved by them.

Ms Leo is loyal and supportive to her chosen mate. Her love, once given, is often a public affair. She likes everyone to know how much she loves you and how wonderful your love is. To Ms Leo her man is the most wonderful person on earth and she expects everyone else to love him as much as she does. If he is the sort who doesn't like being pawed in public, then Ms Leo is not for him. Leo affection is too extravagant to be confined behind locked doors. This lady won't be the other woman, either. She doesn't take kindly to the clandestine, the dishonourable or the second rate – it just isn't her.

She's Number One or nothing. Some Leo ladies of the more insecure kind do take this to extremes, displaying a very unsubtle antipathy to any half-desirable female who hoves into sight and only inviting Plain Janes to their parties. In this, Ms Leo may be making a big mistake, for you can't judge a book by the cover. Ms Leo may be relaxing in the face of a dull exterior, quite blind to the hidden fascination of the inner pages, while her mate is becoming hooked. Leos are not always canny when it comes to emotional undercurrents. Fortunately for Ms Leo, it is rare for her mate to be tempted from her side.

Speaking of insecurity Ms Leo, for all her charm and often very noticeable sex appeal, is by no means always confident of her femininity. This is a secret she may hide even from herself. The truth of the matter is that all of the Fire signs display qualities of assertion and enterprise that we do not traditionally equate with femininity. Thankfully this is at last beginning to change, but there lingers a fear in many a Leo female that she isn't a 'proper' woman and she may hide her dominant tendencies behind a kittenish exterior. Make no mistake, Ms Leo is all woman, and if she's also proud and assertive no man need fear this – only mice!

This lady needs attention, and if she loves a man she needs *all* his attention. He should give her nothing short of adoration and not forget the compliments for they never pall. If he makes her feel truly special, the world takes on a glow for both of them. She also loves to laugh. Her lover should take her to the best places he can afford – later on she will be happy to go 'dutch' for she has a certain independence and pride. It has to be said that Ms Leo can be bossy and pushy – in fact, she's the pushiest in the zodiac. If she has singled a man out from the crowd then she will want him to excel and she may even scan the Sits Vacant columns to pick out a job for him with a higher profile, better prospects or flagrant 'snob value'. If this doesn't suit him, he will have to stand his ground very firmly, without in the least putting her down. He must show he appreciates her help but he has his own way of going about things. There may be some royal rows, but mutual respect and a truce is better than uneasy surrender. Leo woman is better if she has avenues of self-expression of her own, so she is not looking to her mate to enhance her self-esteem.

Ms Leo is an intriguing mixture of fiery unpredictability and fierce possessiveness. Tempestuous and passionate, determined and loyal, she is exciting, challenging but somehow reassuringly reliable, she can make her lover feel like the knight who has won the tournament. He should treasure her for the prize she is and needs to believe she is.

■ LEO MAN IN LOVE

In love, as in most other areas, this man operates along a scale, the one extreme of which is total self-absorption and an obsession with self-importance, the opposite being an unparalleled generosity, radiance and warmth. A woman who is fortunate enough to have the love of one of the 'radiant' Leos should count herself blessed indeed. It is rather more frequent to find Leo males further along the spectrum. Leo is potentially a great egoist, and we are never so vulnerable as in our relationships with the opposite sex. Leo has a vivid sense of hierarchy and wants to be top of the heap.

A woman who is one of the dying breed who yearns for the day when 'men were men and women were glad of it' may find that Mr Leo could be her top dog. Yes, this man is dominant. He likes to be in control of everything, and that probably includes his lover; he likes to shine brightest of all and that means she has to be the jewel in his crown. Further than this, he's always right – that is about everything that's worthy of his interest. His lover may be vouchsafed the superior knowledge concerning egg boiling and bus timetables. Mr Leo never takes a bus anyway – he takes his Bentley. Once it broke down and he did try the bus – his lecture to the bus driver on the Highway Code is something the passengers on bus number 68B will never forget, and neither will his lover.

Like the females of the sign, this man is passionate, loving and committed. He knows, like no one else, how to make a woman feel like a queen. If he's a flamboyant Leo there will be days of wine and roses followed by nights of wine and desire, glitzy events, glamourous parties and love made with unforgettable Leo ardour. If he's the quieter type she will still be left with no doubt that this relationship is in some way out of the ordinary. The poetic undertones and the faraway look convince you of this. Speaking of that look, his lover may not always be sure what he's looking at, least of all thinking about. As with the lovers from all the Fire signs she may have the sneaking feeling that she's playing a part in some drama – so much so that she casts a sneaky look behind to see what's happened to her satin train – or her wings.

Yes, Mr Leo can be a dictator on a power trip. However, he can also be a little boy, more gleeful than Charlie in the Chocolate Factory. In some ways he's an innocent, and one of the easiest men to tease. If he has decided that his lover is 'special' then his ego won't let him believe he's not equally important to her. He doesn't readily change his mind and he's quite hopeless at sensing emotional undercurrents. Equally, he's hopeless at recognising his incompetence in this or any other matter. Add to this a yearning for the poetical and you have a Lion on a choke-lead.

I once knew a Leo man who was in love with an enigmatic and very beautiful woman. Leos are often attracted principally by looks, but there was, in addition, something ethereal about this person. Even on a city street in July she seemed cloaked in medieval mystery. She played 'hard to get', letting it be known she felt strongly for him but couldn't possibly commit herself because her parents relied on her to help look after her crippled brother. After all. 'it wasn't fair to tie him down'. She loved him but 'this could never be', although she would 'die without him' she must leave him free to 'find another', and so it went on. Romantic Leo was completely hooked. He brought her red roses, silk scarves and perfume by the barrel-load. He loved to walk down the High Street with her on his arm, touchingly proud of her love, determined to wait until fate released this noble creature into his arms. This went on for five years. Then one day she was gone. Her parents said she had left for London to join her boyfriend (yes, boyfriend) having found a new and very promising job. Dazed and incredulous, poor Leo was invited into the house, from which he had formerly always been excluded due to the fact that the invalid needed quiet. No crippled brother in sight, Leo sipped his tea and asked after him, fearing the worst. He was greeted by amazement. Yes, Juliet had a brother. He was ten years older and ran a successful publishing business in Ohio. In fact he was due home next week, after five years away . . . .

Needless to say the devastation of this man was extreme, and it was augmented by the humiliation. How many people had known the truth of the matter? Leo was afraid to walk down the street for fear of being a laughing stock. In truth it took him several months even to believe what had happened, let alone adjust to it. It is to this man's credit that the experience did not embitter him, and although he never reached the point where he could laugh at himself he did eventually pick up the pieces and make a happy marriage. Ten years later Juliet came back – unmarried, no longer young, and her 'mystery' faded to a worn and tired air. Leo feels that the hand of Fate was kind to him, in the end.

A woman who enjoys a man who isn't afraid to take charge and relishes being just a little passive on occasion will find that Mr Leo has much to offer her. If it really matters to feel absolutely loved and part of a never-ending drama, and if she is prepared to take care of the budget, the shopping, the cooking and cleaning – in short all of life's mundane details – then Mr Leo could be her hero. It will help if she is naturally in agreement with his dogmas most of the time, and prepared to hold her tongue at others. Harder, perhaps, but equally necessary is a strong sense of her own individuality and the courage to fight her corner with dignity when she has to. If this is you, why then, ascend to the throne and bask in the shaft of sunlight.

■ GAY LEO

Visualise a typical Leo surrounded by stars of stage and screen, sparkling like Liberace and calling everyone 'Darling'. The performing arts may be the favoured milieu for many gays of the sign, and when Leo finds her or himself among the glitterati, then there are few of the problems associated with homosexuality – for whatever the drawbacks of this sort of environment, prejudice is not one of them. Such Leos will find themselves able to express love, affection and desire to members of the same sex with the ardour and openness of the sign.

For Leos in a more ordinary environment things may not be so easy. Leo often does have the panache and the apparent confidence to get away with most things. Some Leos make like filmstars so successfully that everyone tolerates what they may see as the little 'arty-farty foibles'. However, a Leo who is of the quieter sort may suffer considerably. Leos do not like to be disapproved of or despised, and all too often this is still the lot of homosexuals in some sections of the community.

A Leo who is in a position where 'coming out' might mean some form of disgrace needs to learn that concealment does not mean dishonour or shame, but may merely be practical. Naturally, it is much better to find a place where one's preferences may be public, but that may be hard if it means the sacrifice of a lucrative job or your house or flat. It is a truism, but worth remembering that a real friend will stand by you whatever, and you are worth better company than that of those who might disapprove.

■ LEO LOVE TRAPS

Drama queens and kings

Leo is one of the signs that falls in love with love. For Leo there has to be something happening or else it's just all too boring and playing solitaire isn't Leonine style – even if it's a large and flawless diamond solitaire. So, if the 'girl I love's not here I'll love the girl that's near' becomes Leo's motto. No, this doesn't mean that Leos will be unfaithful, for there's enough drama, pathos and poetry in an absent love to keep them going for quite a while, especially if the letters are frequent and the phone calls lingering. In a sense, Leos' love is never far away, for they hold the image in their big, imaginative hearts. However, if there's no love 'here' in any sense, then Leo becomes fed up and lonely, and that's the flashpoint for an unsuitable romance with what is 'near'. Leo can then capitalise on the drama of it all, the agony and the ecstasy. There may be temper tantrums, breaking up and making up, declarations and heart searching. These are par for the course in many Leonine relationships anyway, when they may distract from real feelings. These could be feelings that are really petty, and which the Lion would far rather not own up to, such as resentment. When it's an 'in love with love' affair then the storms distract from the fact there is no real feeling present.

This is a difficult matter, for with Leo, as we have seen, a little fantasy is necessary and certainly doesn't denote an unsuitable match, so it may be hard to recognise when imagination has extended to unreality. With their penchant for flattery Leos can be a pushover for the sincere and insincere alike. Besides, Leos aren't slow to commit themselves. 'Marry in haste, repent at leisure' was the old saying. How can Leo avoid 'repentance'?

As a Leo you need to remember that while you may express your feelings you must hold back on the promises. Amid all the sound and fury you must take time to consider what you truly feel and whether this person is really going to suit you, some years down the line. Nothing can take away the feelings at the moment, but the best rule is enjoy this time if it is enjoyable, weather it if not and resist the temptation to force the issue or to make commitment. Good wine will only improve with keeping.

Jewels in the crown

Frankly Leo can be a downright snobbish sign and this may emerge in relationships as a selection of a partner on the basis of looks, status or money. Leo then feels his or her own importance is enhanced, but Leo has simply 'collected' this person as an adornment. This isn't good enough and will leave Leo feeling empty, stuck with a paltry fake instead of a diamond. Many Leos do this at some time in their lives, but a Leo who does it repeatedly is probably one who is insecure. Why do you need a partner who looks like a film star or drives a flash car? Aren't you good enough yourself? Toss that Leonine mane and have some self-respect.

■ LEO AND MARRIAGE

This sign is one of the 'marrying kind' and of all the Fire signs Leos are best at long-term relationships. Children, too, are often important to Leo, although Mrs Leo may well choose not to have a large family because she wants a career and interests of her own. Of greatest importance to Leo is that the children should not supplant him or her – the partner still comes first and Leo wants to remain the most important in the partner's eyes, also.

Leos need a mate and you are very forlorn indeed when lonely, although you may manage to be stoical. Once the knot is tied you are usually faithful, especially if your partner manages to flatter you sufficiently and keep a little magic alive in the relationship. Leos are extremely possessive, although you aren't given particularly to suspicion. You react in an uncompromising manner when you feel a rival is at hand, but you are often wrong in this, and in truth fairly easy to deceive. Leos aren't good liars, though bluster often gets you through a tight corner. Although you can't be bothered to have an affair, if moderately happy, you are great flirts and like to believe that every member of the opposite sex finds you devastating. In this Leo often shows a double standard – it's okay for you to invite attention but woe betide a partner who attempts the same!

As marriage partners you Leos are delightful, irritating, eternally entertaining, warm, bossy and reliable – in regard to your presence, that is. Regarding most other things, you tend to leave life's boring details to your partners. For some that's fine, for others disaster. Make sure you know how your partner feels about this beforehand, because he or she won't get the Lion to change!

■ WHEN LOVE WALKS OUT – HOW LEO COPES

There is one word for this – badly. You cannot take rejection – it leaves you bewildered. There is no sadder sight than a bereft and lonely Lion. At first there may be tears and lots of bluster. You may make excessive demands on the sympathies of friends, trying to get emotional balm. The need within you for attention and consolation is tremendous at this time, but trying to meet it is like filling a bucket with a hole in it. Nothing can mend this great, broken heart.

Alternatively, you may be overcome with hurt pride and draw away to lick wounds in private, possibly denying that this silly person meant anything at all. Or you may throw yourself into relationships or activities that soothe your pride, pretending nothing has happened. Others shouldn't be fooled, but should leave you alone for a while. A Leo whether sorrowing noisily or 'into denial' may also go into a deep depression. You need this time alone, in your own depths, to get a sense of perspective and to recover, but you should not be left alone too long, for you may disappear into the 'black Sun' version of Leo, radiating darkness and despair. (The black Sun is potentially a transformative symbol, relating to the hidden journey of the Sun beneath the earth. But when the black Sun consumes, dawn never comes, and Leo remains unredeemed in the Underworld.)

After a while you should be coaxed back out into the sunshine with a few compliments and promises of good times. You may demur a little, for after all this has been the Tragedy of all time and everyone must know this. Sooner or later you will thaw, however, and the big cat will learn to play again.

Starting afresh

There is a danger that a recovering Leo may launch him or herself into another relationship rather too quickly. Certainly Leo does need something at this point to make him or her feel good. It is far better if this can be supplied by friends who are wise and kind, and who know what to say. Leo may also look for an ambitious and creative project in which to get absorbed, and that is a very good idea.

Leo is a sign that might be called 'strong' in many senses, but Leos do not always recover quickly. Remember no half-measures with the Lion. If you have loved someone your self-esteem may not enable you to admit you were wrong about the person, and that can leave you in a sorry position. Some Leos sulk for years – this is to be discouraged.

You Leos need to realise that you are important in and of yourselves, because your confidence may be only skin deep. You also need to tell yourselves that we are all wrong sometimes, and making a mistake does not make you a fool. Sooner or later you can manoeuvre yourselves into a position where you pity the foolishness of the one who has left you – after all, look what he or she has lost! Then Leo really is on the road to recovery.

■ PRACTICE AND CHANGE ■

- Try to keep a sense of perspective in relationships. Remind yourself that you do tend to go over the top and protect yourself from hurt.

- Do not be too ready to commit yourself in any big way until you are quite sure. No, you cannot be sure after two weeks, however it may feel. Give it time.

- Try not to expect too much of yourself and partners. Let the flames die down a little and do not be anxious, for they will rekindle – no one can keep at maximum perpetually.

- Always keep romance alive by regular candle-lit dinners, surprise outings, unexpected gifts. Make sure your partner understands your need for this, too. It certainly isn't about being mercenary. Your partner will appreciate this in time.

- Try to relax about rivals. No one can take from you what is rightfully yours, and you will be even more attractive if you remain a little aloof at times.

- Outer impressions are important to you, but don't be taken in by appearances when it comes to lovers. Good looks and money are no substitute for a pleasant and interesting personality – but you know that really, don't you?

3

All in the family

He that plays the king shall be welcome

Shakespeare, *Hamlet*

Those who have a Leo in the family will probably know it! Leos can be playful and funny, having the whole family in gales of laughter, or they can cast a cloud over everything with their moods and demands. Let us take a look at Leo in some of the traditional family roles.

LEO MOTHER

This mother is proud and doting. She does tend to expect a lot from her children and will want them to be a credit to her. How she visualises this will depend upon her own standards. Often it is appearances that are important. Some Leo mothers are so proud they will never let their children appear in anything second-hand, which makes this a very expensive family indeed. With others it is academic achievements that count. Leo mother will spend a great deal on private lessons, and nag a lot, to make sure that little Jack or Jill is top of the class in something. Alternatively, there may be lessons in drama, music or dancing. The children of Leo must shine, and this may occasionally be a burden, if it gets out of hand.

On the other hand, while Leo mother may push her children, she can rarely see anything wrong in them. She is loyal and fiercely protective. Leo mother can be quite indomitable, and if she is proved wrong she will simply lift her chin and ignore it. In the privacy of the home, however, the Leo mum can be a strong disciplinarian and quite inflexible once she has discovered a transgression.

Leo mother does not like to be supplanted by her children. It will wound her immeasurably if her partner seems to love or care for them more than he does for her. She must always be Number One. No mate of a Leo should come home with a toy for the child, without having a bunch of flowers for Mum, in the other hand. At heart she is eternally a child – and do remember that word 'special'. Never treat anyone near her as more special than her for an instant – even the children she has produced.

The Leo mum is often very playful and will readily leave chores to enter into the games of children, whatever their age. She does this gracefully and quite without self-consciousness. She's great at planning parties and outings – everything done with style. Everyone likes to be invited, for her parties are lavish and great fun.

Motherhood is rarely the pinnacle of life to this lady. She may well find it all too mundane and limiting. She badly needs a career herself and some outlet for her creative talents and her need to shine. As with anything she does, she does her best in motherhood and she will put her heart and soul into the process. However, the banality of it all may be brought forcibly to her attention with her first child, and so it may be her last. It isn't characteristic of Leo mother to struggle with a large family, unless she can afford full-time help. On the odd occasion when Leo does throw herself into the role of 'little woman' she is quite likely to exert pressure and control on her family to achieve all the things she secretly wanted for herself, and she may become quite a matriarch. It's not easy for her children if Leo mum's seeing the drama teacher to try to get them the lead part in the school play if they feel they'll just die if they have to go on stage. Likewise, her children may want to learn carpentry or dressmaking, but woe betide them if Leo mum has her sights on RADA or one of the top universities! Far better for the Leo mum to have her own theatre in which to shine – then everyone else can enjoy life along with her and bask in her enthusiasm.

This isn't a mum to confront head on, for she is the firmest, stubbornest and most determined in the zodiac – and sometimes she takes rebellion very personally. However, she is deeply warm and loving – and open to flattery. If her children pay her a few compliments, buy her a box of her favourite chocolate and make her laugh with some jokes she knows they have memorised just for her, they can choose their moment to make their request. She loves them so much she'll never refuse!

■ LEO FATHER

Leo dad loves to play 'paterfamilias'. He needs to be looked up to and he loves his advice to be sought. Usually he will have a special chair, and he will greatly appreciate being brought cups of tea or more interesting treats by members of the family.

Of course, this man is always right. It doesn't do to argue with Leo dad – not necessary either. It isn't hard for his children to get their own way, as with Leo mum, but they must have more sense than to make this obvious. Leo dad loves to give lectures and he may seem stern, but actually discipline isn't his style. He would far rather go out and play ball and show off to his children's mates – this can be embarrassing, but often he's so entertaining he's the neighbourhood favourite and his children feel proud.

As with Leo mum, this man likes to be proud of his family, but as he rarely has the bulk of the childcare he may also relish a large family. To some Leo men this enhances their masculinity. Of course, he must never take second place to the children and will feel inwardly forlorn if his wife is too fraught and preoccupied to give him a kiss when he comes in and cook a special meal on his birthday. He's playful and entertaining – he may love to come home with treats that set the whole family gasping 'Oh, thanks, Dad!' and he often puts a great deal of energy into arranging family events. Leo dad may well bring out the home movies or the puppet show to brighten up a wet weekend – however, he may also be too busy to spend as much time with his family as he, and they, would like, because he is usually ambitious at work. The result of this may be children who are perpetually longing for their charismatic daddy, who so rarely has the time to be with them.

Leo father is often as ambitious for the children as his female counter-part and he must take great care not to push them. It is very hard for him to accept that he doesn't know what's best for everybody, let alone his own children, and one of his greatest tasks as a parent is to learn to respect the individuality of the children, for they are not actors in a play that he is directing. This aside, Leo dad is often larger than life, fascinating and funny. He makes the world seem like an exciting place, and that is a great start in life.

■ THE LEO CHILD

If ever anyone can manage to look regal sitting in a highchair with spaghetti all over his or her face, this child can do it. However, along with that one-year-old dignity goes a streak of pure tyranny.

This child should not be crossed lightly, for she or he has a will of iron and a temper like a supernova – unless there are many planets in a more reserved sign. Even then, young Leo is wilful. The truth of the matter is that we do not give children sufficient credit for knowing what is good and necessary for them. We are all apt to inflict adult standards without asking ourselves if this really matters. So what if little Leo insists on orange juice on the breakfast cornflakes and has taken an inexplicable aversion to the cardigan that Nanny knitted for Christmas? There is nothing about the nutritional elements of orange juice that need concern a caring parent. As for the cardigan, aren't the feelings of the little one just as important as Nanny's? And would *you* wear something you didn't like? Say the cat unravelled it, and go for a quiet life with young Leo.

From the earliest age try to show this little person that you respect his or her wishes, as far as possible. If you do decide that something really is important enough to make a stand, try to avoid confrontation and appeal to vanity, where possible. And when the chips are down, dig your heels in and don't budge. Leo will respect you for this, and will eventually learn that you cannot be browbeaten. You'll feel like an emotional punchbag, but hang on in there – this kid will give you many proud moments in years to come.

Never tell young Leos not to show off. Encourage them to develop skills that will eventually be genuinely entertaining to others. Meanwhile appreciate what they do and give tactful suggestions for improvements. Capitalise on whatever skills seem apparent. Deft with fingers? Buy the child a magician's kit. Good memory? Then she or he can learn poetry, jokes or stories. Dancing, music, performing arts – all these are Leo favourites, but for the Leo who is more introverted, plenty of stimulation for the imagination and the intellect is called for. Most children love to have stories read to them, and none more so than Leo.

Please do not ever demean or humiliate your Leo child, especially in public. This is a cruel thing to do to any child (or indeed adult) but for Leo it is especially hurtful and damaging. A Leo who has been put down may well grow into the 'black Sun' type of Leo, who can be extremely cruel. Such a person seeks out the weak spots in others in order to feed his or her own ego and sense of power, which has been damaged by humiliation and poor treatment. What your Leo child needs is a healthy sense of his or her own capabilities, dignity and responsibility. The old attitude that children need 'taking down a peg' should be tossed on a bonfire. People need to feel they are valuable and unique, and someone who is confident in the sense of self enhances the identity and self-respect of all who come near, for he or she has a strengthening quality. This applies to no one more so than Leo.

When the storms of adolescence appear on the horizon you will have to hold on to your hat! Leo falls in love six times a week, and there will be tears and ecstasy alternating in bewildering succession. Do not try to cramp the style of the teenager. Do your best to help him or her look as glamourous as possible and give encouragement in the development of their sexuality. This is common sense and will get the teenager on your side – hopefully – so that your words of caution will be treated with respect. Leos are not always good judges of character, but don't try to tell them that! Gently discourage commitment at too early an age, not by criticising the beloved but by pointing out all the interesting other things life may have to offer to a young person of such ability. Emphasise the dangers that strangers can pose, making it clear that Leos may be a special target because they are so attractive. Explain without scaremongering that unwelcome attention isn't at all flattering and may well be extremely demeaning. For instance, a young female Leo may find the attentions of the opposite sex quite delicious, and may have too much confidence in her ability to control the situation with queenly aplomb when she might, in fact, be in real danger. When handling such situations always remember never to put Leos down or call into question any of their abilities. Tell it like it is, tell them you know they are too sensible to take chances, and chauffeur them everywhere that you can. Adolescence – thankfully! – doesn't last forever.

In time you will be rewarded by the appearance of a confident and dignified adult.

■ LEO AS SIBLINGS

It must be said that Leo as an older sibling can be awfully bossy. It is good to give Leos some real responsibility (don't give them messy chores – they will resent it, but they should still pull their weight), and older Leos can be encouraged to look after little ones. They need to understand that being older and wiser (hopefully) means responsibility, not the right to command. If Leo has been well treated, he or she should learn sooner rather than later how to treat those who are younger.

Your older Leo brother or sister will delight in explaining all the 'facts of life' to you, and, if you flatter them enough they will happily help you with your homework. Remember never to tell stories about them in front of friends for they will hate you forever if you make them look foolish. Leo will usually come to your side if you are threatened and may well become angry to the point of violence in your defence.

As younger siblings Leo can be more troublesome for they tend to challenge everything, and it may be hell if you are left to look after them. Again, flattery is usually the key, and if you make Leo feel good enough they will eat out of your hand.

Leo brothers and sisters can really light up the family scene, and if you find them a drag just think how funny they were playing cha-rades last Christmas, how they saved up six weeks' pocket money to buy you a birthday present, and how they confronted your Maths teacher who was going to give you a detention for not doing your homework. 'It's not fair,' said Leo, 'he had a headache.' So you both ended up in detention – but what the hell! Worth putting up with that bossy know-it-all really!

◼ LEO IN THE HOME

Leos do not like to be confined and they will sometimes spread their possession over the entire house as if they own every corner! It is hard for a Leo to cope with little space, because it is against the Leonine nature. Your Leo youngster should be given as much space as possible. Sometimes this may mean other family members get less, but it should be made clear that this isn't favouritism, for everyone has different needs, and other priorities may be called for in the case of your Piscean child, for instance, who may well value privacy in a small nook, rather than being able to spread out.

Of course, the reality is that many of us have to cope with much less space than we would like. With Leos try to make sure that their own area looks imposing, even if it is small. Mirrors can give the illusion of space and a large window will help greatly. This is a sign that needs light. Leo won't want to bother with fussy bits and bobs, so a built-in cupboard into which everything can be thrown is better than lots of little shelves and drawers. Make sure there is a sizeable noticeboard somewhere in the house to exhibit early artwork, because Leos are very proud of anything they produce.

While every effort needs to be made to accommodate the expansive nature of the Lion, when it comes down to it Leo has to make the best of things, like the rest of us, and it would be wrong and unrealistic to give him or her special treatment – this could encourage excessive egotism in later life and could be almost as damaging as repressing Leo. The best idea is to include Leo in as many decisions as possible, from as early an age as possible, including that of organising the living space. That is the best way to help Leo come to terms with realities – not easy for any of the Fire signs – and to deal with them in a creative fashion.

■ PRACTICE AND CHANGE ■

- Leo mothers need their own creative outlets. If you are a Leo parent do not imagine that this will fulfil you entirely by itself. When parenthood arrives you will want to put your heart and soul into it, but do not expect too much of yourself. You will be a better parent if you have your own modes of self-expression.

- As parents you need to remind yourselves not to push your children too hard in any direction.

- In family situations you Leos need to remind yourselves that you must give and take, and that it is more important to you to concentrate on what you can contribute rather than trying to rule the roost. Other people also are individuals.

- Leo must never be demeaned. This will lead to problems later. A Leo who has been respected will respect others.

- It is best to include all family members in decision making in a 'family council'. Leo especially will respond to this approach.

- Leos love anything theatrical and amusing. Group family entertainment should be organised. Leos have the gift of showing others how to enjoy themselves – give Leos the opportunity to do this.

- Leos take a great pride in their families – remember a family of lions is called a 'pride'. There is something in Leo that can lift family life above the commonplace. Treasure this.

- The art with Leos is to help them to recognise that the views and individuality of others count, without crushing them. Leos must learn a little humility, but their heads must never be bowed.

4 Friendships and the single life

*I cast my own warmth around me and
it is reflected in others*

Anais Nin

Of course, friendships are important to all of us, whether we are in a steady relationship or single. However, when we are single we often have more time to devote to friends. Friends are so important to Leos that while they may put a great deal into their partnership they usually leave ample time for socialising.

LEO AS A FRIEND

You Lions are usually party animals. You like to live it up at the centre of a crowd, you love a circle of admirers to impress – yes, you like an audience. However, although you seek popularity, you can be very loyal friends. This is not generally a superficial sign, although it is generally a dominant one! Leos like to be the benefactors in a friendship. You do not take kindly to receiving charity. Friends shouldn't turn out their old baby clothes for the new Leo mum or give you a shirt that doesn't suit you with the remark 'I've only worn it once'. They won't get many thanks for that. If they know their Leo friend is in need – emotional, financial or whatever – they should invite you to dinner with company you can sparkle in and let slip information about job opportunities and the like, so you can act as if the idea was yours in the first place. A lonely Leo won't mind if friends do a little matchmaking – after all, everyone should at least have the chance to get close to the Sun! However, friends shouldn't meddle too much after that. If it's going to happen, then it will. Leo isn't one to miss a golden opportunity.

We have said Leo is loyal. You will stand by friends in adversity and may be very generous with your time, money and every other resource. Unfortunately you are also generous with your advice and may become quite impatient if friends don't see the sense of what you say and *do* it! Leo will sort everyone out from birth to death – there, it's all quite simple. The Lion will sit back with an air of satisfaction, having taken no notice of any little hangups or obstacles, let alone friends' personal preferences. Leos are tremendously helpful, positive people and you certainly can make friends feel that there is an answer to everything. However, empathic you are not. You do not have a bone in your whole body that knows simply how to respond to sorrow, how to 'be' with it and sympathise without trying relentlessly, and rather unrealistically, to brighten it up. You can be brilliant companions if friends are down or depressed but if they have problems that are subtle, deep and complex you can be irritating in the extreme. Every Leo does need to learn that some things cannot be sorted, you cannot command away the pain of another, and that sometimes the simple gift of your sunny presence is enough. A Leo who can remember this is a treasure indeed.

Yours isn't an especially tactful sign. If a friend's new green coat makes him or her look like something on a day outing from a morgue, you will tell the friend. However, you are often less than open about your own feelings, especially when these might appear 'infra dig'. Leo never likes to look petty. You may find a mutual acquaintance irritating in the extreme or you may be jealous of them. Rather than admit it Leo may make everyone's life a misery by being irritable and superior. Like many people, you Leos do need to be very open about your feelings. If you are a Leo and you recognise yourself here then remember that it is best to work out and face your own feelings before someone else gets there first. Some people are very intuitive and will know why you are acting a certain way before you do – you wouldn't want anyone to be one jump ahead, would you?

Leo is a competitive sign and this applies also where friends are concerned. It has to be said that Leo is often a dreadful snob! Friends of Leos can feel complimented that they have been deemed good enough. No matter how much their Leo friend likes them, Leo will rarely permit them to upstage him or her. A Leo who I used to know spent six months deciding on the colour scheme for her new kitchen. Having at length settled on a design she really liked she found that someone else she knew had quite independently chosen virtually the same. She told me that now she would have to start all over again. 'Why?' I enquired, bemused. 'It's what you wanted and it's not as if you're copying her – you made up your own mind beforehand.' 'Oh no,' she said disdainfully, 'I couldn't!' Enough said. A Leo who goes to such extremes may be sacrificing her own uniqueness for an individuality that is more apparent than real. Being 'one up' can mean that Leo is way down on being herself.

Leo friends can add sparkle to the lives of those who know them. Wherever they are it seems as if the Sun is shining, and all sorts of things are possible. You Leos do need to remind yourselves that you can't sort out everything and everyone. You also must remember that if you beat your friends at their own games you will lose them. Your great gift is your positive attitude and personality plus. Those who have a Leo friend should appreciate him or her for this and all the entertaining qualities, and should be generous with Leo when he or she has to be best at everything. Put it down to the irrepressible child within.

■ LEO AND THE SINGLE LIFE

You might assume that such a fun-loving person, so popular, cheery and confident, would find nothing but a round of razzamatazz in being single, making whoopee day and night – but you would be quite wrong. Leos just hate being alone. They hate it worse even than Cancers – although they might be less willing to admit it, and they are even more lost than Libra without a mate.

Of course, there are benefits in being single, especially for the younger Leo. Without a partner there may be more time and opportunity to sample life and to seek out the places and situations that are most entertaining. However, it is rare for you Leos to see this. Your image of a partner isn't someone who cramps your style, but rather of someone to tag along and support you. Leos love to have someone to come home to.

However, being single does have much to offer you and it is quite important that young Leos do not commit themselves too soon. Leo needs to experiment, for there is a 'wild side' to the personality. They need the time to indulge the untamed parts of themselves. By this I do not mean just sexually. A Leo who has had the opportunity to live it up is less likely to become a demanding, unreasonable partner.

Another benefit in being single is that Leo may find the solitary life more conducive to self-exploration. As a Leo you often need an audience to convince you not only that you are special, but almost that you exist. This may sound strange for such a strong sign, but in Leo a true sense of identity may be lacking and you may always be measuring yourself by the cheers and appreciation you receive. The roaring Lion may be more like a paper tiger, a papier-mâché Sun that looks gaudy but crumples in on an empty centre when pushed. In the long run, you are never truly convinced that there is anything at your core unless you discover it for yourself. The way to finding this may be hard and lonely but it is certainly worth it. In the long run you may shine in rather a more subdued fashion but with more vibrancy, constancy and purpose.

■ PRACTICE AND CHANGE ■

- Leo's great gift in friendship is your cheery, confident presence. You should restrain yourself from finding answers, giving advice and pushing.

- While you may love compliments and pretty clothes from exclusive boutiques, try also to accept thankfully humbler offerings from friends. Not everyone assesses value in the same way as you. It really is the thought that counts.

- Be aware that you may be competing with friends, and not all of them may take kindly to it. Ask yourself what is more important, their company or outshining them. You may have to dim your brilliance a little if you do not want to be lonely.

- You can be a snob – admit it! It is fine to be selective, but ask yourself whether the standards that you are applying are truly important.

- How much are you really worrying what people think and what impression you are giving? When you think about it, isn't that rather beneath you? Having the courage to be yourself will give you more true personal presence in the end.

- Try to make the best of time alone in some way. Devote your time to something creative that is just about you. What have you always wanted to do? Make yourself do it just for you, no one else, no audience.

5

Career

A man can succeed at almost anything
for which he has unlimited enthusiasm

Charles Schwab

Leos love to be supreme in all walks of life, but this is often especially evident in their career. Leos need to be noticed, to achieve prominence and acclaim. Prestige is possibly more important to Leos than authority, but they are not averse to both.

Naturally, there are the most subdued representatives of the sign, who do not appear to seek the spotlight. However, even Leos who are doing something fairly mundane are likely to make something important of what they do.

■ TRADITIONAL LEO CAREERS

Two important words to remember in connection with Leo occupations are importance and playfulness. They may seem almost mutually exclusive, but they are not. Leo careers include:

- dancer
- actor
- teacher
- youth worker
- jeweller
- managerial positions

- sportsperson
- prominent work in the media
- general performing arts
- social organiser
- overseer

Generally any occupations to do with entertainment, games or creativity and anything that involves taking a broad view and projecting a sunny, confident and commanding persona will suit Leo. Many Leos tend to favour either the playful side – some gift-of-the-gab salespeople have a strong Leo, and Leo is *the* sign of theatre – or the more authoritarian, such as managerial roles. Whichever, a place behind the scenes rarely suits them, unless it is a pivotal place.

■ WHAT TO LOOK FOR IN YOUR WORK

Of course, the truth of the matter is that the great majority of people work in large insurance corporations, sales offices, shops or factories. Relatively few of us can choose a profession, train for it and find a fulfilling lifestyle, and as time progresses this is becoming more elusive.

To help you find a job that suits you, you need to bear in mind the spirit of what is recommended, not the specific occupation. One office job is not like another, one clothes shop may differ enormously from another down the street in terms of environment and opportunity. If you are a Leo you need to make sure of several things when seeking employment:

● There is either something intrinsically special about this job, or it has scope for you to leave your mark and make it special. You must be proud of what you do.

● You will have some scope to make your own decisions without someone breathing down your neck.

● There is possibility of advancement of some kind, not merely financial – although that is important. You should feel there is opportunity for greater prominence and decision making.

● You do not feel there is anything sordid or shameful about your working conditions – nothing that may make you feel depressed or demeaned.

- Your work is not too rigidly defined. There should be encouragement of creative input from you, so you can really make this job your own.

- There is some opportunity for 'play'. This could be lavish lunches on some occasions, the necessity for 'dressing up' or looking your best, a swish company car – or something about the job itself that is 'playful', for instance if you were involved in designing computer or board games.

So there is no need to feel that you have to look for a specifically Leonine job. Many Leos would hate the detailed work of a jeweller and are far too indolent to contemplate even a game of squash at lunchtime, let alone play professional sport! Look for something that suits in content and atmosphere, rather than its label. If it doesn't suit, don't hang around too long trying to make changes and battling with the status quo. Move on.

■ PRETENDER TO THE THRONE

We have heard much about the Leonine need to feel superior, to occupy positions of authority and influence and generally to be 'somebody'. So what happens to Leos who are managers *manqué*, who never make it halfway up the ladder, let alone to the top? What do they do? They pretend.

The 'Pretender' is always middle aged or older, and most often male. Women are in the sometimes fortunate position of having a greater variety of outlets. Ms Leo may find her place in the sun arranging the church flowers or chairing the bridge club. Mr Leo, who has worked all his life and achieved mediocrity still often has only his job. Some Leos become withdrawn and disdainful, but the Pretender does the opposite – he makes like the MD, has a pompous air and wears gold jewellery (which he can ill afford) and orders the office juniors around in a loud voice, especially when there are customers or members of the public within earshot.

The Pretender can be a most obnoxious and irritating person to encounter when you join a company because he may humiliate you and have you doing menial jobs if he gets the chance. The management will back him up to the hilt, because he's an institution – he has his uses, and any threat to his authority might mean a threat to theirs – that is, until they give him early retirement. The answer to the Pretender is subtle flattery, a sycophantic smile and a secret sense of humour and pathos – for this is a pathetic figure.

The good thing about the Pretender is that he has his generous side. On his birthday he never forgets to buy cream cakes and a bottle of champagne or stand everybody doubles at the bar after work. The Pretender deserves everyone's pity for he is really living in a fantasy land, because reality cannot be born – and one day he may have to face the terrible fact that he's nobody.

If you recognise characteristics of the Pretender in you – whether you are fifteen or fifty-five – wake up and get a life. What are you, a paper Sun? Come now, every Leo can find a way to be truly special. What are your interests? Why not become an authority on the subjects that fascinate you? Why not develop yourself? Why not have the courage to look outwards, and break the empty shell that has become your life? Only by waking up to reality can you build a dream that's real, and I know that as a Leo you can do it.

■ THE STARLET

Most organisations have one or two of these dazzlers, always looking like something from the pages of *Vogue*, flashing their 1,000-watt smile and apparently carrying all before them in a blaze of glory. Often they are employed in some high-profile area such as sales, advertising or PR. Glamourous, lively, with the entrée to all the high spots in town, these people seem tailored especially to make 'ordinary mortals' feel as relevant as yesterday's newspaper. Sickening, some call it. Others go glassy eyed with admiration.

Very much a 'textbook' Leo, the Starlet is a type of pretender, too, only she or he is still enjoying it, still 'going somewhere'. If you are lucky enough to be a golden girl or boy yourself, then by all means revel in it – but do remember that there is more to life than this and the glitz will leave you empty eventually, unless you get into something deeper, like what life is really about and what you, as a Leo, are going to do with it. If the Starlet leaves you feeling like a fieldmouse, then aren't you being negative? Surely the fact that someone is enjoying life with all its opportunities should be an inspiration to the rest of us, not a burden. The idea that the generosity of the universe is limited is largely fostered by our own self-doubts – everyone can find their own special niche. And if the Starlet dazzles you then you are being taken in by appearances – there is more to life than that.

■ THE LEO BOSS

Those who have a Leo boss should be prepared to lay their best ideas at this person's feet and have them annexed. Leos are great plagiarists and never more so than when in a position of authority. This is their least endearing trait. Apart from that, there is much to recommend following in the wake of the King of the Beasts.

The Leo boss is dynamic. His or her panoramic version often doesn't take in details – that's what employees are there for. Leos often can't see the trees for the wood, but they usually have the sense to find 'a person who can'. Employees will need to get used to dotting the i's and crossing the t's for Leo, mopping up, organising and offering their own creative input on the altar of Leo's ambitions. As a reward they will probably receive generous pay and bonuses, compliments, opportunities and a free advice service. This may sound patronising, but an influential Leo can be very useful. If employees are a little late, because they had to Interflora a bouquet to their sick friend or buy a special outfit, Leo may well understand – unless it's one of Leo's off-days. The best Leos aren't interested in the letter of the law, but the spirit – and the 'spirit' of the Lion-law is that others give him or her 101 per cent, that they think of all the petty details Leo has missed (because Leo's secretly a bit confused by them) and that they treat Leo as if he or she really is the monarch of the urban jungle. Compliments go a long way with this boss.

Yes, Leos can be demanding, unappreciative and condescending. They can also be warm, generous and endlessly helpful. If employees are ambitious they could go far with this boss for they are *en route* for 'top of the heap' – that is, if they are going to be content as second fiddle. If they want to lead their own orchestra, sooner or later they will have to part company – chances are they're Leos themselves!

■ THE LEO EMPLOYEE

If an employer takes this person on in a menial role – say as office cleaner or errand-person – the employer should at least try to give Leo a title. Hygiene Manager or Communications Executive will mean more to Leo, than an increase in pay, and it will get the best out of them. Leo employees know quite well that they aren't going to stay at the bottom, and they will respond to their boss's tacit recognition of the fact. Above all, an employer should never, *never* rebuke a Leo employee in front of anyone else, unless the employer really wants Leo to leave at the first opportunity. Leo can't bear to be humiliated in public.

An employer should always notice the things that Leo does well and remark upon it. When new recruits arrive let Leo train them if at all possible – no one blossoms like a Leo with a little authority. Show Leos you appreciate all their innovative ideas, for they may have many, and try to implement some, for Leo has a grasp of wide perspectives and may cut through all the details previously thought of as impenetrable as a barbed-wire fence. Leo hates rules and regulations, so employers should not be pedantic about these. If Leos are appreciated no one will be short changed by their efforts. Trust their sense of responsibility and they will blossom. Please do not expect Leo to work in conditions that are squalid, dark or dreary, for they will become extremely depressed. Some Leos are shy and don't really seek a high-profile position, but make no mistake, they have pride and aesthetic sense in abundance.

Leos often like a fairly lavish lifestyle, so salary should be generous, for although Leo rates position above money, the latter still goes a long way. We all like to feel appreciated, but Leo needs it as much as the daily vitamins. If employers always remember this, their Leo employees will never cease to reward them.

■ WHEN UNEMPLOYMENT STRIKES

To Leo this will be difficult in proportion to the amount of status dependent on the job. For a Leo who has put her or his life into an occupation, this is nothing short of tragedy. Leo doesn't take well to change, loss of face is a nightmare and poverty is a spectre that chills the proud Leonine heart.

If you are a Leo facing this situation remember that what you are losing is your job, not your Self. All the talents and attributes that got you where you were are still yours to command. Indeed, it is quite possible that you weren't operating at maximum potential, because although you like success you also like security. Were you hanging on to something second-rate rather than risk making changes? Well, maybe fate has done you a good turn. Naturally, you will feel frightened – you can admit this to yourself if to no one else. However, what you must now do is muster all your drive and launch yourself into the process of job finding. Compile a portfolio of all your attributes, positions held (running a drama club, scout group or whatever) and achievements, however small these may seem.

If your job was one that you really loved and that did answer all of your requirements, naturally you will need to mourn the loss of it. Don't put on a brave face. It will take you a while to get over this. However, in time get over it you most certainly will. After a short interval, gird up your loins and take the steps mentioned in the paragraph above. It was a job – an enjoyable, rewarding job, yes, but a job. You are still *you*, you still have the same gifts and abilities to bring to bear elsewhere, so get out and find a place for them.

■ SELF-EMPLOYMENT AND OTHER MATTERS

Not all work relies on a company and an employer, for there are many other approaches. Leos are tailor-made to run their own business or to work freelance – indeed, most Leos do, at some time, consider the possibility of going it alone. However, there are a few points to be borne in mind.

First, as a Leo you are unlikely to be a loner – you were born to lead, not to stride out in splendid isolation. Sooner or later you will need to be working in close contact with others (who give you the proper respect, of course!) or you will need to have people who work for you. Second, there are two things that you are not good with – that is, unless you have a substantial amount of Earth in your natal chart. These two things are money and regulations. All too often Leos starting on their own borrow lavishly and set up in plush premises before they have adequate backing. You must moderate this impulse if you are to succeed, or have a partner who will keep you in check. Also you will need to obtain the advice of a good accountant from the word go, or taxation and other conundrums may catch around your ankles like jungle creepers.

■ PRACTICE AND CHANGE ■

- Leos need some prestige and plenty of appreciation, whatever their employment may be. You have a right to seek this.

- No Leo should be expected to work in sordid surroundings for you find this unutterably depressing and will not be able to give of your best. Avoid this like the plague.

- You always need scope for advancement.

- Leonine creative potential is considerable. While you may not be good with details you can often see the broad landscape and deserve to be listened to, even if you are inexperienced.

- Many Leos are very inventive in establishing a special niche in what might be termed quite ordinary posts. You should be encouraged to be yourself, and if this involves giving advice to all and sundry you should, if possible, be respected. You should aim to be an 'authority' on something.

- For Leo there must always be scope for 'play', for it is stimulating to the imagination. Does your day include this?

- Ask yourself if the job you are doing truly answers that urge within you to be 'special'. If not, do make plans to change this, because it can corrode your brilliance and leave you dissatisfied and bitter in time. Make changes now.

6 Healthy, wealthy – and wise?

A light purse makes a heavy heart

Sixteenth-century proverb

■ HEALTH

Astrological observations on health are often quite difficult, even when based on the entire chart. For health is a complex matter, dependent on emotional, as well as physical, matters and affected by the habits we develop in life. What may we usefully say about the health of Leo in general?

Leos are not given to half-measures, and because of this they may go to all sorts of extremes. This may include eating and drinking too much at times. Also these big-hearted people are extremely sensitive and can be deeply hurt, which takes its toll on vitality, especially as Leos will often try to conceal their misery. Although not prone to depression on a regular basis, when they do get down Leos may 'go for a whopper' on occasion. Naturally, this will lower their resistance to infection.

In common with the other Fire signs it may be hard for Leos to admit when they are tired, hungry or overwrought. It is all too easy for them to ignore their bodies until it is too late, and they may thus court a complete physical – and sometimes emotional – breakdown. Some Leos seek physical excellence of some sort and may push themselves to the limit in an effort to transcend the confines of the body. All Leos need to remind themselves that their bodies are precious, that they have needs and limitations, and that their bodies will serve Leo best if they are taken care of. Leos usually have excellent constitutions and great recuperative powers, but they still need to look after themselves.

Stress and strain

The ill effects of stress are well publicised. Because Leo is an ambitious sign, determined to excel in all undertakings. Leos often put too many demands on their bodies. Leo traditionally is said to rule the heart and the spinal column.

Heart disease is a modern epidemic, and while there is certainly no statistical reason for Leos to fear they are more at risk of heart attack than anyone else, it is worth bearing in mind that high living and high expectations are often implicated in this disease. Leos often like rich food, which does not help the problem.

Each Leo should be aware that while you may reach for the skies you must keep both feet on the ground – and nowhere is this more necessary than in the matter of health. You should turn your enthusiasm and energy into the process of healthy living in order that your splendid vitality can be maintained and channelled to the best advantage.

You need to play hard in order to relax, and must cultivate sensible habits of resting and nutrition. Leos often like to 'cat-nap': if this is your preference then make time for it in your daily schedule. You will feel much better for it.

Because Leo is a 'fixed' sign your opinions and habits may be rigid, despite the fact that you are often innovators. Yours is a stubborn, unbending sign, and this may be reflected in back troubles. Leos who are 'stiff-necked' with pride may find they are indeed stiff, physically. This may result in complaints such as arthritis or rheumatism. Again, regular exercise and a relaxed attitude are something for which all Leos should make provision.

■ MONEY

Among the many talents of Leo we cannot number financial expertise. That is, Leo is quite as capable as the next person of adding two and two, and even better at adding two hundred thousand to two hundred thousand! Sticking by these figures, however, being limited by them is another matter entirely and it may be very galling indeed to you not to be able to go and buy what you want because the wretched figures don't add up. Many Leos gaily ignore such piffling trifles and run up bills all over town with devil-may-care grandiosity. Such a Leo often has someone else, somewhere, picking up the tab and going grey with anxiety. And for some Leos the whole pack of cards comes tumbling down, burying them in financial disaster. Of course, not every Leo is this extreme. Some are good budgeters. These are either Leos who have a goodly amount of the Earth Element in the birth chart, or Leos who have learnt – often the hard way.

Leo really does hate a life of deprivation, and the sordid truly can make this sign dysfunctional, if not quite ill. You need to remember that while temporary denial may feel most irritating, utter ruin will be a dreadful humiliation. You need to use your considerable imagination, not to blind you to the facts but to cast your mind forwards to what it will be like in the future if you continue to be unrealistic with money. It will be bad – very, very bad.

So, if you want to live like a king you have to wise up. Earn the money first, be inventive and enterprising, make your time count, don't waste time on schemes that aren't going to pay, and don't run up bills because you will be paying out on interest long after you should have inherited the kingdom. If you want a little style and comfort without delay, go for a job that offers a company car and, if possible, an expense account. Don't spend what you haven't got – exercise your powers of control in financial matters. Plan a little for some cut-price glamour. Remember what we said earlier about the magic of candlelight? Good wine won't break the bank. Ask for the silk tie or underwear for your birthday – and dream and scheme to your heart's content about that wonderful time to come when you will be able to walk into Harrods and buy the place up!

■ WISDOM

I doubt if there is a Leo who doesn't believe he or she is pretty wise and that they have gems in their head that everyone should have the benefit of hearing. Many Leos are one-man or one-woman advisory services on just about everything, from the care of gerbils to the price of shares. Leos just love to be respected and looked up to for 'knowing a thing or two'. Because Leos have considerable breadth of vision, often they do indeed know a thing or two thousand.

However, true Leonine wisdom doesn't concern anything that you can give advice about, to anyone. It comes from knowing and realising the nature and potential of the Self, from earnestly exploring deep within and becoming acquainted with that inner spark that we may call 'the Divine'. A Leo who has achieved consciousness of the eternal Self, in whatever way he or she conceives it, is one who has achieved wisdom and strength far beyond the temporal. Such a Leo 'knows' at a level quite beyond conceit. She or he may well be worth following in some respect – all the more so because such a Leo is unlikely to mind whether anyone follows or not.

■ PRACTICE AND CHANGE ■

Health

● Although Leo is a 'larger-than-life' sign, you do need to aim for moderation when it comes to personal habits. It may be a good idea to ask yourself in which areas you are pushing yourself too far, and ease up.

● Leo needs play – this can't be stressed too often. When is your playtime? Make time for a regular one, doing something just for the joy of it.

● Leo may need to cultivate a little flexibility of attitude. An unbending nature will be reflected in similar posture, which in time may lead to back and other troubles. Learn to chill out and loosen up.

Wealth

● You may need to learn that extravagance will eventually bring you to the very thing you dread – penury and humiliation – and to take steps to avoid this. One way may be to tie up a portion of your salary in investment.

● There isn't anything magic about credit cards, they are merely a passport to synthetic glory that you will pay for many times over in the end.

● Use your imagination to supply some glamour which does not cost the earth. Also focus that imagination on times to come when you really will be wealthy – because you are working and planning right now.

7

Style and leisure

The busiest men have the most leisure

Nineteenth-century proverb

■ YOUR LEISURE

Anyone who has ever seen a family of cats or lions at play can have no doubt that these are the most playful creatures. A kitten running after a ball of string is a fur-ball of enthusiasm. Then the little creature rolls over on to its back, paws in the air – could there possibly be anything more endearing? But go to stroke that furry little tummy and you may find your fist in a nest of claws. Leos are rather like this. They are full of innocent enthusiasm, but they are fiercely competitive and have just a hint of wildness about them, at times. It quite often gives them the competitive edge.

Leos may put a great deal of energy into work so you need absorbing play. Competitive sports sometimes appeal. You hate anything amateur and so may prefer to confine yourselves to what you are good at, but if this means you do only your work, you need to remember that 'all work and no play makes Jack a dull boy'. Besides, relaxation will improve your performance at work. Leos generally enjoy many forms of theatre. This can involve going to the theatre or cinema or taking part in amateur productions, which you may direct or in which you may play the lead. Often Leo makes a good youth leader and so you may like to devote some spare time to Guide companies or Scout packs. Organising any club or society that captures your interest is a good pastime, and you usually carry the post of Chairperson majestically.

In addition, Leos need to cultivate the knack of 'basking'. All cats do it, from the mighty lion to the tiny kitten – no one can relax like a cat. This is one feline trait that does not always come easily to Leo, however, for while you may know how to lounge gracefully you may be anything but relaxed inside. Leos should use the benefits of sauna or massage to give sheer, sensuous delight. You also should try to budget for luxurious treats – something that makes you feel really indulged. This could be oysters and wine, a session in a Jacuzzi or a weekend at a health farm. It doesn't really matter what – it's pressing your luxury button that counts.

In general, Leos aren't terribly good at hobbies, because a hobby is, almost by definition, something you dabble in, and while your efforts may be interesting, even quite good, they may not reach a standard of excellence. This may send you into a self-defeating pattern, so that the process is anything but relaxing. The intellectual Leo who does a little woodworking to amuse himself or herself may go cross-eyed, measuring umpteen times and ending up sawing in the wrong place through sheer fatigue. Leos who are painting in their spare time may screw up their efforts in despair, because they aren't Picassos. Leos need to learn to ease up on the perfectionism for a while. Hobbies aren't about excellence. Yes, you want to do the best you can, but the object of this is to stimulate your imagination and to *enjoy*. Remind yourself that this change of perspective and relaxation will make you even better at your 'day job'.

Finally, Leos can be great escapists and may thoroughly relish a film that depicts the sort of grandure and romance they would like to live on a daily basis. Similarly they can become lost in books. If it has a larger-than-life theme then it's worth a try for Leo. Curl up and enjoy.

Holidays

Leos do like to have a holiday that they can boast about to their friends. This sign has more than a streak of snobbery, and a weekend in Clacton just won't do. The more exotic, expensive and unusual the better. Yes, Leo does have a sense of adventure and you like the challenge of the unknown. You like a little one-upmanship even more, it has to be said. Coming back with a glowing tan and a flamboyant something from the bazaar does you a treat. Even better if you can be photographed at Cannes with Kevin Costner in the background! Leos are sometimes attracted to well-known glamour spots such as St Tropez, Monte Carlo or Las Vegas. More subtle Leos may like to visit the Far East. Wherever, Leo does love a holiday – if you can get time off work, where you are, of course, indispensable, that is! Holidays are special occasions, when Leo is in her or his element.

If Leos do not live in a warm part of the world they will probably seek the sun. This sign is ruled by the Sun, and while most of us are envigorated by a bright, sunny day there is something about sunlight that is very beneficial to Leo. They need it, to recharge their batteries. Of course, we all know that too much exposure to the Sun can be very dangerous, but Leos don't have to sunbathe in order to get the benefits. Looking out upon a sunny vista from the shade, watching sunrise and just being somewhere where there is not a cloud in the sky for a fortnight can be very uplifting to your spirits.

■ YOUR STYLE

This should be dramatic and luxurious. Most Leos are unsuited to the drab, or even the subdued. Yes, there are Leos who do not like to blare their presence out upon the world, but even these will usually avoid the second-rate or shoddy. Colours should be bright, vibrant and rich. Some Leos do like to overload themselves with jewellery; more subtle Leos still like to display something incredibly expensive on finger or wrist. Many Leos are trendsetters – not always of the zany type, but individualists, nonetheless. This sign does like to feel pampered and Leos may be the dream of every beautician. From the crown of your heads down to the tips of your wonderfully manicured toes, Leos may display the sensuous, regal grooming of Cleopatra's court.

Leo living space needs also to have an 'air' about it. You may like exotic ornaments, deep-pile carpets and generally a faint air of the splendour of seventeenth-century Versailles. 'Luxury' and 'majesty' are your keywords. However, there are also Leos who don't much notice their surroundings. They are preoccupied with higher things and they certainly don't like housework – although they may force themselves to do it, being an energetic sign that dislikes squalor. Leos often like their dwelling to be imposing, if they can afford this, and they do like plenty of space, where this is possible. The occasional bit of rich embroidery or original painting is likely to adorn the walls. Leos like things to be in the best possible taste, comfortable and of noticeably good quality.

When you are choosing purchases for yourself or your home think quality, dramatic, luxuriant, bright, cheerful, generous, opulent, rich, individual, warm, beautiful. Often you will spend more than you can afford – be prepared to draw in your belt later. You don't usually buy on impulse, but will often weigh up the pros and cons of a purchase, and feel mortified if someone else has chosen the same thing. For that reason you may choose to shop at distinctive boutiques. Also ensure the shop will accept returns just in case you find the Joneses have got there before you!

■ PRACTICE AND CHANGE ■

- Make sure that you set time aside for hobbies and pastimes. You may need to get used to not being terribly good at what you do – this is just for the fun and relaxation, which you need. Not only will hobbies be good for you, they will also enhance the creativity of your ordinary life, so they are worth the trouble and the time, whatever angle you take.

- Instead of wanting to be 'the best', concentrate sometimes on being 'the best you'. Competing against yourself can be less of a strain. However, competitive sports are good for you, for they loosen up the body and ease tension. Just don't overdo it.

- Do have a holiday, even if you can't afford anything smart. I'm sure that you can make even an ordinary place sound fascinating. Soon all your friends will be wanting to go to Southend-on-Sea, to see how marvellous it is!

- Make sure that you do have time in the sun, when possible. Sunny pictures – even a plaque of the Sun itself, such as you often find in 'New Age' shops – can be heartening to have around.

- If your decor is unsuitable you will become depressed – anything drab can even make you ill. It is worth putting effort into pleasant, bright surroundings.

- Some Leos are fairly careless about their looks, perhaps feeling life is too full to bother with details. More typically, you will want to create 'an impression', however muted this may be. Whenever you make a purchase give yourself a quiet moment to ask 'Is this *really* me?' Never mind the fashion, or whether it's good for work. You won't shine in anything that isn't your style.

Appendix 1

█ LEO COMBINED WITH MOON SIGN

Our 'birth sign' or 'star sign' refers to the sign of the zodiac occupied by the Sun when we were born. This is also called our 'Sun sign' and this book is concerned with Leo as a Sun sign. However, as we saw in the Introduction, a horoscope means much more than the position of the Sun alone. All the other planets have to be taken into consideration by an astrologer. Of great importance is the position of the Moon.

The Moon completes a tour of the zodiac in about twenty-eight days, changing sign every two days or so. The Moon relates to our instincts, responses, reactions, habits, comfort zone and 'where we live' emotionally – and sometimes physically. It is very important in respect of our intuitional abilities and our capacity to feel part of our environment, but because what the Moon rules is usually non-verbal and non-rational; it has been neglected. This has meant that our lives have become lop-sided. Learning to be friends with our instincts can lead to greater well-being and wholeness.

Consult the table on page 81 to find which sign the Moon was in, at the time of your birth. This, combined with your Sun sign is a valuable clue to deeper understanding.

Find your Moon number

Look up your month and day of birth. Then read across to find your personal Moon number. Now go to Chart 2, below.

January		February		March		April		May		June	
1,2	1	1,2	3	1,2	3	1,2	5	1,2	6	1,2	8
3,4	2	3,4	4	3,4	4	3,4	6	3,4	7	3,4	9
5,6	3	5,6	5	5,6	5	5,6	7	5,6	8	5,6,7	10
7,8	4	7,8	6	7,8	6	7,8	8	7,8	9	8,9	11
9,10	5	9,10,11	7	9,10	7	9,10,11	9	9,10	10	10,11,12	12
11,12	6	12,13	8	11,12	8	12,13	10	11,12,13	11	13,14	1
13,14	7	14,15	9	13,14	9	14,15,16	11	14,15,16	12	15,16,17	2
15,16,17	8	16,17,18	10	15,16,17	10	17,18	12	17,18	1	18,19	3
18,19	9	19,20	11	18,19	11	19,20,21	1	19,20	2	20,21	4
20,21	10	21,22,23	12	20,21,22	12	22,23	2	21,22,23	3	22,23	5
22,23,24	11	24,25	1	24,25	1	24,25	3	24,25	4	24,25	6
25,26	12	26,27,28	2	26,27	2	26,27,28	4	26,27	5	26,27	7
27,28,29	1	29	3	28,29	3	29,30	5	28,29	6	28,29,30	8
30,31	2			30,31	4			30,31	7		

July		August		September		October		November		December	
1,2	9	1	10	1,2	12	1,2	1	1,2,3	3	1,2	4
3,4	10	2,3	11	3,4	1	3,4	2	4,5	4	3,4	5
5,6,7	11	4,5,6	12	5,6,7	2	5,6	3	6,7	5	5,6	6
8,9	12	7,8	1	8,9	3	7,8,9	4	8,9	6	7,8,9	7
10,11,12	1	9,10	2	10,11	4	10,11	5	10,11	7	10,11	8
13,14	2	11,12,13	3	12,13	5	12,13	6	12,13	8	12,13	9
15,16	3	14,15	4	14,15	6	14,15	7	14,15,16	9	14,15	10
17,18	4	16,17	5	16,17	7	16,17	8	17,18	10	16,17	11
19,20	5	18,19	6	18,19	8	18,19	9	19,20	11	18,19,20	12
21,22,23	6	20,21	7	20,21,22	9	20,21	10	21,22,23	12	21,22	1
24,25	7	22,23	8	23,24	10	22,23,24	11	24,25	1	23,24,25	2
26,27	8	24,25	9	25,26,27	11	25,26	12	26,27,28	2	26,27	3
28,29	9	26,27,28	10	28,29	12	27,28,29	1	29,30	3	28,29	4
30,31	10	29,30	11	30	1	30,31	2			30,31	5
		31	12								

Find your Moon sign

Find your year of birth. Then read across to the column of your Moon number. Where they intersect shows your Moon sign.

Birth year	1	2	3	4	5	6	7	8	9	10	11	12
1900 1919 1938 1957 1976	Ari	Tau	Gem	Can	Leo	Vir	Lib	Sco	Sag	Cap	Aqu	Pis
1901 1920 1939 1958 1977	Tau	Gem	Can	Leo	Vir	Lib	Sco	Sag	Cap	Aqu	Pis	Ari
1902 1921 1940 1959 1978	Gem	Can	Leo	Vir	Lib	Sco	Sag	Cap	Aqu	Pis	Ari	Tau
1903 1922 1941 1960 1979	Can	Leo	Vir	Lib	Sco	Sag	Cap	Aqu	Pis	Ari	Tau	Gem
1904 1923 1942 1961 1980	Leo	Vir	Lib	Sco	Sag	Cap	Aqu	Pis	Ari	Tau	Gem	Can
1905 1924 1943 1962 1981	Vir	Lib	Sco	Sag	Cap	Aqu	Pis	Ari	Tau	Gem	Can	Leo
1906 1925 1944 1963 1982	Lib	Sco	Sag	Cap	Aqu	Pis	Ari	Tau	Gem	Can	Leo	Vir
1907 1926 1945 1964 1983	Sco	Sag	Cap	Aqu	Pis	Ari	Tau	Gem	Can	Leo	Vir	Lib
1908 1927 1946 1965 1984	Sag	Cap	Aqu	Pis	Ari	Tau	Gem	Can	Leo	Vir	Lib	Sco
1909 1928 1947 1966 1985	Cap	Aqu	Pis	Ari	Tau	Gem	Can	Leo	Vir	Lib	Sco	Sag
1910 1929 1948 1967 1986	Aqu	Pis	Ari	Tau	Gem	Can	Leo	Vir	Lib	Sco	Sag	Cap
1911 1930 1949 1968 1987	Pis	Ari	Tau	Gem	Can	Leo	Vir	Lib	Sco	Sag	Cap	Aqu
1912 1931 1950 1969 1988	Ari	Tau	Gem	Can	Leo	Vir	Lib	Sco	Sag	Cap	Aqu	Pis
1913 1932 1951 1970 1989	Tau	Gem	Can	Leo	Vir	Lib	Sco	Sag	Cap	Aqu	Pis	Ari
1914 1933 1952 1971 1990	Gem	Can	Leo	Vir	Lib	Sco	Sag	Cap	Aqu	Pis	Ari	Tau
1915 1934 1953 1972 1991	Can	Leo	Vir	Lib	Sco	Sag	Cap	Aqu	Pis	Ari	Tau	Gem
1916 1935 1954 1973 1992	Leo	Vir	Lib	Sco	Sag	Cap	Aqu	Pis	Ari	Tau	Gem	Can
1917 1936 1955 1974 1993	Vir	Lib	Sco	Sag	Cap	Aqu	Pis	Ari	Tau	Gem	Can	Leo
1918 1937 1956 1975 1994	Lib	Sco	Sag	Cap	Aqu	Pis	Ari	Tau	Gem	Can	Leo	Vir

Ari	Tau	Gem	Can	Leo	Vir	Lib	Sco	Sag	Cap	Aqu	Pis

Leo Sun / Leo Moon

You probably have a very 'sunny' nature and a deep need to be the centre of attention. Usually you have the courage of your convictions and a great deal of faith in life. When you go down it's probably with a bang, but rarely for long. Generally you need to work at being more realistic – you can be something of an idealist. Also it has to be said that you can be bossy! You are an innovator and a leader, but you are also a playful person, loving to explore all the available possibilities in life. You love to be loved, but your secret may be that you don't really love yourself, and when the applause of the crowd dies it may leave you feeling very empty. You need to learn ways of feeling good about yourself, of finding emotional nurture that does not depend on the admiration of others. Discover the magic of self-exploration and be your own star and audience. It's all you need.

Leo Sun / Virgo Moon

Because you have a rather self-critical core, you may be very sensitive and have a deep need for the limelight, in order to feel 'special'. You can be your own worst enemy, because you may get caught in fussing about details and feel very frustrated that you are not involved in something more large scale. You have a passion for excellence – you like things not only to look good, they must *be* good. On the plus side, you have the practicality and eye for detail to help underpin your schemes, and you are capable of some impressive results in your chosen spheres. Remember that you do not have to be perfect to be loved, and most important of all, learn to love yourself, warts and all. Your best motto could be 'Analyse in moderation and don't agonise – organise'.

Leo Sun / Libra Moon

You are charm itself. Your cheerful, positive nature and good manners can gain you popularity and influence. Although you often appear relaxed you are actually capable of achieving a great deal. It is very important to you to be thought well of, and while you seek to be top of the heap, you do not like to feel you have put anyone's nose out of joint – you would far rather be loved by all. Beautiful and stylish surroundings are vital to you and you prize peace – but not at any price. Sometimes you can be strangely argumentative if you feel things need stirring up. In general, you prefer to ignore more disturbing factors, such as unacceptable feelings, and you like to think you are above all that sort of thing – but you aren't. When people disagree with you or become upset, you need to ask yourself whether, despite your politeness, you haven't been insensitive to true emotion. Most of all, use your sense of fairness to listen to all sides of yourself. You may have troubled feelings that need a hearing.

Leo Sun / Scorpio Moon

No half-measure with you! You are an intense and passionate person, with a possessive streak and a strongly sexual side. Proud and stubborn, once you have made up your mind about something it may be impossible to deflect you. You may hide your vulnerability by creating storms and making demands – you probably have a sense of the dramatic. You are a very resourceful person, capable of surprising achievement. While you love to create an impression, you are slow to trust and would rather die than have you inner feelings exposed. Sometimes you feel pulled apart inside, needing to give the impression that you can cope with anything, and yet having inner needs that are most poignant. You are a powerful person – use that power to confront yourself and achieve true, lasting satisfaction.

Leo Sun / Sagittarius Moon

You are one of the playgirls or playboys of the zodiac, with an optimistic disposition and an immense faith both in yourself and in life. You may be a literal gambler. More often you gamble with life, following your hunches – and often winning. Status is very important to you, and you like people to look up to you for your panache, personality and general wisdom. Your sense of humour is probably lively, but that will not extend to times when the joke is on you and your dignity is compromised! Although you come across as very warm, in effect it may be hard to get close to you, and you may have a habit of telling people what you think and then being amazed when they take offence. Freedom is deeply important to you. Learn to give emotional freedom to others by validating their feelings – similarly to yourself, for you may escape from true feelings into search for meanings. Cultivate also that real freedom that comes from willingly doing what must be done.

Leo Sun / Capricorn Moon

You are probably a profoundly ambitious person. It is not enough for you to be respected, you need some real power in terms of practical decision making and material assets. The standards that you set for yourself and others are no doubt very high, and you need to be aware of the stress this creates in you. While it is very hard indeed for you to admit vulnerability, you do crave approval, and while you are busy meeting standards you may not stop to ask yourself who set them. Do they really meet your needs? It may be hard for you to feel secure, for part of you is very cautious while another part demands the limelight – sometimes you may feel that you have exposed yourself. Discover your own true needs and standards – that way lies the greatest security.

Leo Sun / Aquarius Moon

Certainly you are an individualist. You are aware of yourself as a unique, important being but you also instinctively seek to be part of a group, to be detached and friendly to all, rather than self-seeking. You are likely to be pulled two ways and may sometimes embarrass yourself by attention seeking. At the same time you are aware of the importance of individuality and are continually striving to balance the two. Your intuitions may be strong and you should take note of your dreams. Your task is to experience fully the power of your self-hood and to integrate it with the needs of the group. In so doing you should not reason yourself out of any feelings you may have that you consider 'ignoble'. Learn to be a true friend to yourself rather than sorting out other people's problems, for that may be a way of avoidance. Freedom is very important to you, so set free your emotions and discover more about your own true path in life.

Leo Sun / Pisces Moon

In all probability you are a warm-hearted, open-handed person, and while you are able to give the impression of confidence, you are also deeply sensitive. You are able to sense what a person truly needs and may be able to turn up with just the right gift, say just the right thing at the right time. Your displays of generosity are more than pure theatre – but you do have your theatrical side. To you everything is sometimes very much larger than life, fairytale, tragedy, comedy too – but never commonplace. You have the gift for mythologising. Real life may be almost unbearable to you and you have a great need to get lost in something that is much greater and more 'divine'. Although you have many talents you may be afflicted with discontent. Learn to nurture yourself in common-sense ways, for you may be missing these in your dreams, preoccupations and rescue missions.

Leo Sun / Aries Moon

Generally you are forthright, confident and sometimes hot-headed! You take the attitude that you can achieve anything you want with-out help from anybody. Sometimes you ride roughshod over the opposition in your conquest of life. You can be demanding and bossy – something of a crusader and entrepreneur. You are con-cerned with goals, possibilities and stimulating ideas rather than spadework, and you may rush off to start something else before you have finished the job in hand. While searching for excitement you may be missing real feeling, having lots of experiences but never truly savouring anything. You need to differentiate between the impulse of the moment and your own more long-term needs, and to realise that you, like all of us, have needs and vulnerabilities. In this way you can develop a more solid sense of reality, so that the many seeds you sow have opportunity to take root.

Leo Sun / Taurus Moon

Comfort and stability are important to you and you like to own beauti-ful things – and people! You know how to enjoy life and can do this flamboyantly at times – at others, your style is more intimate. This can communicate itself to other people who feel warmed by your pres-ence and sense that it is OK to enjoy themselves. You do not readily let go of anything – relationships, partners, ideas – and your greatest faults may be that you can be stubborn and dogmatic at times, sticking to your point of view and even evangelising. Self-esteem and dignity are important to you, and you like to feel self-sufficient. Underneath you may be truly terrified of letting go, moving on. Thus you may become entrenched in habits that are not good for you, which will undermine true self-esteem. You will feel better about yourself if you develop healthy, balanced habits and faith in your own resourcefulness that enables you to meet change when necessary.

Leo Sun/Gemini Moon

You are able to satisfy your need for attention by your amusing chatter and brilliant ideas. You are very resourceful and can come up with clever plans to underpin your ideals. Busy, playful and imaginative, you stir up your environment with your dreams and schemes and you can be a stimulating companion. You may not like to confront your feelings, and when you are hurt or your ego is dented you may escape from this into rhetoric or intellectualisation. You do possess a reflective quality, but you may still be focussing on matters that are outside you, rather than concentrating upon what is within. When you bring the laser of your intellect to bear upon your real essence, feelings and purpose in life, and when you give yourself permission really to feel, rather than just talking about it – that is when life will become truly exciting.

Leo Sun/Cancer Moon

Familial concerns are no doubt important to you – and if you don't have many blood relatives then a sense of family among your friends is likely to figure. You may play Big Mamma or Papa, but secretly you hope that others will fulfil your needs. Sometimes you may be quite touchy, for you are both proud and sensitive and you may feel very insecure if you cannot possess someone you love. At

Appendix 2

▪ ZODIACAL COMPATIBILITY

To assess fully the compatibility of two people an astrologer needs to have the entire chart of each individual, and while Sun-sign factors will be noticeable there is a legion of other important points to be taken into account. Venus and Mercury are always very close to the Sun, and while these are often in the Sun sign, so intensifying its effect, they may also fall in one of the signs lying on either side of your Sun sign. So, as a Leo you may have Venus and/or Mercury in Cancer or Virgo, and this will increase your empathy with these signs. In addition the Moon and all the other planets including the Ascendant and Midheaven need to be taken into account. So if you have always been drawn to Capricorns, maybe you have Moon or Ascendant in Capricorn.

In order to give a vivid character sketch things have to be stated graphically. You should look for the dynamics at work, rather than be too literal about interpretation – for instance, you may find that you do not have much difficulty with Taurus, but you may be aware that they are coming from a very different 'place'. It is up to the two of you whether a relationship works, for it can if you are both committed. Part of achieving that is using the awareness you have to help, not necessarily as a reason for abandoning the relationship. There are always points of compatibility, and we are here to learn from each other.

On a scale of 1 (worst) to 4 (best), here is a table to assess instantly the superficial compatibility rating between Leo and companions:

Leo 3	Aquarius 1
Virgo 1	Pisces 3
Libra 4	Aries 4
Scorpio 1	Taurus 2
Sagittarius 4	Gemini 3
Capricorn 2	Cancer 2

■ LEO COMPATIBILITIES

Leo with Leo

Here we have two Suns shining blindingly. Are you ready for a binary system or will there be a continual struggle to see who eclipses whom? It is likely that you will be perpetually competing for the spotlight. Neither of you gives way, each is proud and stubborn – and (whisper, whisper) very needy. The question is whether you can find your big hearts and sense of humour or whether each turns the cold shoulder and the Ice Age returns.

As lovers Lots of drama and passion. Each of you expects a lot and each of you gives a lot – the trouble is that neither of you is very realistic. The plus here is that you can enter each other's fantasy world with gusto, and you are loyal and protective of each other. Ms Leo rejoices that at last she has found a man who understands how to live, while Mr Leo readily sees that this is a lady who can be a credit to him. The trouble can be that this relationship is all chiefs and no Indians. Who is going to make the subtle observations that can soothe and heal if you are both intent on rulership? Who will be tactful, sensible, compromising – and who will do the washing up? Yes, this can work, but each of you needs to cultivate self-awareness and a respect for the other's individuality, which should be achievable.

As friends Naturally, you will share lots of interests and may hold each other in high esteem, feeling that there is no one quite like this loyal, sunny friend. Your friendship could endure for many years.

As business partners For this to work you need more sober input, so wheel in a Virgo or Capricorn. You are both creative and imaginative, but your unbridled spending will threaten the success of your venture.

Leo with Virgo

Fire and Earth often attract, and so these signs that have so little in common may be inexorably drawn to a shared hearth and home. In fact, you are the perfect complement to each other, but you need to work very hard at understanding and respect. Virgo, as usual, may feel that he or she is doing all the dirty work – which is probably literally true as well as metaphorically – and may become so wound up and impatient that he or she leaves – much to the surprise of Leo, who is then bereft. Virgo is an excellent backdrop to Leo style, but Virgo needs appreciation and Leo needs to be free of fussing, at least some of the time.

As lovers Sex between you could be great. Virgo takes a while to warm up, and this could inflame Leo's enthusiasm. Ms Leo admires this man's impeccable eye for detail, and she appreciates how this could enhance her own style. Mr Leo is fascinated by this cool lady who knows just how to dress – her slightly untouchable air yet quiet sensuality can be a real turn on. Leo may feel frustrated sooner rather than later by Virgo's insistence on detail, while Virgo may be somewhat frayed by Leo's grand sweeps that threaten to smash all the best china. If this relationship survives at the start it could well go the distance.

As friends Virgo has the perfect approach when it comes to planning out all the Lion's ideas, although in so doing some of them may be nit-picked out of existence! Leo may sigh and look long suffering, knowing Virgo is worth it!

As business partners You will have many initial differences, but if you can get this off the ground it has much going for it. Leo has style, imagination, flair, big ideas and no idea at all about money. Virgo has common sense, method, organisation and planning. Virgo holds the purse!

Leo with Libra

Here we have two 'beautiful people' who enjoy socialising. Other chart factors considered, this is likely to be a high-profile partnership, with stylish parties and outings. Libra is very accommodating and will often give way to the Lion's bluster without losing face, while Leo may satisfy some of the Libran's ideals of what a partnership should be like. However, the truth can be that all the socialising, or external interests may divert from the fact that there is little real intimacy here.

As lovers Attraction may be strong at the start. Ms Leo is charmed by the manners and bearing of Libra, while Mr Leo finds the style and grace of Ms Libra irresistible. However, Leo isn't one for half-measures and the sheer fire and passion of the Lion may be a bit much for this Air sign that prefers to talk and think about the value and essence of the relationship, rather than become consumed in it. Nonetheless, Libra at least gives the impression of being able to live up to the Lion's high standards of romance and passion, while Libra respects the commitment of Leo. A true emotional bond may be elusive, but Libra might not mind and Leo – with the right ego massage – might not notice.

As friends This is likely to work out beautifully and you will have fun planning visits to the theatre, entertaining together and generally appreciating and enjoying life. Leo provides just the stimulus Libra needs, while Libra cools things down enough to make them workable.

As business partners This could pose problems. You may design impressive premises and look as if you're making millions, while just puffing clouds of hot air. Lots of dash and no cash, for you are both extravagant. Leo has brilliant ideas and can organise on a large scale. Libra is great at charming people. Get an Earth sign on board for practicality.

Leo with Scorpio

Depth and drama, passion and intensity, this is a make-or-break relationship. You are both fiercely proud, both possessive and both stubborn – and you both expect 101 per cent in a relationship. You see much to admire in each other and this could be an exciting relationship, if you can each stand the strain.

As lovers This can be a real earthquake. Leo is demonstrative, open and demanding, and while Scorpio is much more secretive an explosive response is just below the surface. Mr Leo is enthralled by the depth and enigma of Ms Scorpio, while Ms Leo admires the sheer power exuded by the Scorpio male. However, both of you are very touchy, and while Leo may rant and rave and throw a rather childish tantrum, Scorpio recedes. Where there was fire there is now ice and Scorpio weaves a spell of emotional manipulation that makes the Lion thrash about in an invisible web. What can help the situation is mutual respect and a reminder of what initially attracted you. Scorpio may have envied Leo's openness and innocent self-exposure, and Leo will have been drawn to Scorpionic subtlety. It's what you wanted and it's what you got. Talk, communicate and work at understanding.

As friends   Without the sexual spark you may dislike each other on sight. On the other hand, you could forge a relationship where there is fierce loyalty, understanding and mutual protectiveness. Scorpio shows Leo depths the Lion hadn't bothered to acknowledge, while Leo offers Scorpio a passage to openness and faith. There may be lots of 'deep and meaningfuls' when the Lion hits a bad patch, while Scorpio, when in the glooms, will get whisked out on to the town.

As business partners   Not bad, if you can get through the rumpus. Scorpio is cautious and intuitive; Leo is enthusiastic and expansive.

Leo with Sagittarius

You two should understand each other very well and have an instant rapport. Sagittarius is the joker, the wild card of the zodiac and Leo may find Sagittarius great fun to be with. This relationship can really take off in a big way, but it could crash and burn because no one knows how to come in to land or cope with the basic necessities of life. Sagitarrius loves Leo's playfulness, but might not want to come up with the goods when Leo seeks commitment.

As lovers   Here there may be lots of sound and fury but little substance. Fantasy runs high in all the Fire signs, but getting down to basics may be too banal and somehow the initial promise isn't played out in the sack (or the mountaintop or aeroplane WC). Ms Leo certainly appreciates that Mr Sagittarius has ideas that are big enough for both of them, while Mr Leo finds the energy and adventurous spirit of Ms Sagittarius galvanising. However, Leo requires wholehearted commitment at some stage and is also prepared to give it, and it is at this point that the Archer may disappoint.

As friends This may work better than a sexual relationship. You share an immense zest for life and are likely to have some great adventures together. You can set the town alight, plan wonderful parties with a pavilion, fireworks and waiters (but do stop to work out the finances, please!) and go off on impromptu trips to who-knows-where. You both like to live life to the full and if you share interests, whether hill walking, sky diving or UFO spotting you will put lots of energy into it.

As business partners Rather too much of a good thing, big on ideas and minuscule on practicality, unless there is some Earth in your charts. Sagittarius may disappear with a wave, leaving a very angry Leo to clean up and pay up!

Leo with Capricorn

Fire and Earth again, and the attraction may be strong. You share a deep need to progress in the world and to achieve esteem, although you could hardly have more different styles. Capricorn is worldly wise, unobtrusive and utterly determined on advancement; Leo is ebullient, innocent and showy. Capricorn may feel that the Lion expresses something from deep within his or her own heart, that never finds the light of day, and Leo may appreciate that Capricorn is going somewhere and Leo wants to come too. The alternative could be that neither has any patience with the other.

As lovers Passion often runs high between Earth and Fire, and you are both highly sexual beings in your way. Capricorn is generally very at home with her or his body, and this solid sensuality can be reassuring to Leo, of whom the same is not true, although there may be much flamboyant expression. Ms Leo finds this man cool and capable and does her best to impress him, while he gives enough appreciation to keep her interested. Mr Leo finds this impeccable lady very tantalising. He wants to warm her up, but at a deeper level senses that some of his 'boyishness' might be safe here. Trouble can come later when Capricorn gets fed up with clearing up after Leo, paying the bills and coping with the big-headedness, while Leo may find Capricorn frustrating, dogmatic and dull. Much depends on whether the two of you can hang on to the initial respect and admiration and say '*Vive la différence!*'

As friends You may feel you have nothing at all in common. Leo calls Capricorn a wet blanket, while the Goat despises all that bluster. On the other hand, Capricorn has a talent for implementing the Lion's schemes, and Leo can galvanise Capricorn.

As business partners Excellent, with tolerance. Give the purse to Capricorn!

Leo with Aquarius

You are two zodiacal opposites. Where Leo is concerned with personal development, Aquarius is preoccupied with group concerns. Aquarius is detached, Leo is involved; Aquarius tries hard to be unselfish while Leo is unashamedly self-centred. Each of you complements the other and you may see much to admire, or to despise. The truth is that in many ways you are alike – dogmatic and self-righteous, and with a fun-loving streak.

As lovers The attraction may be strong, initially, but Aquarius cannot match the intensity of the Lion, and with neither a very passionate emotional content nor a sensual one, the relationship could become platonic. Ms Leo admires the humour and quirky approach of Mr Aquarius, while Mr Leo finds this individualistic lady very intriguing. However, Leo always wants to be boss, and while Aquarius is much less obvious about this, he or she will tend to monopolise the moral high ground and dominate from there.

This can result in perpetual conflict, as both of you are stubborn. However, Leo can learn broader perspectives from Aquarius, and Aquarius may find ways to develop that electric individuality. Be prepared to learn from each other.

As friends You may irritate each other intensely, or you may sense that the middle ground could be fertile. If you share ideals and drives, yours could be an effective and dedicated partnership. You find each other entertaining and can share many a good laugh.

As business partners Here there could be lots of arguments, for each of you will be sure that your own ideas are correct. Each of you is likely to have plenty of ideas but neither of you is that good on details. Aquarius has a sense of duty and may resentfully pore over accounts while Leo swans around. Best to divide tasks as clearly as possible.

Leo with Pisces

There is much that attracts the two of you, for you share a certain dreaminess, although Piscean dreams are much more fluid and other-wordly than those of the Lion. Pisces has a world-weary tinge that may seek to dilute Leo's fizz, while Leo becomes perplexed and impatient at Piscean vacillations. Nonetheless, Pisces is adept at the ego massage that Leo needs, and there is something deeply reasurring to Pisces in the fire and staunchness of Leo.

As lovers Emotions are likely to run very high and there could be a magical quality to this romance, with sex hitting the transcendent. Pisces has the subtlety to deal with unspoken Leonine insecurities quite unobtrusively, while the sheer passion of Leo is a great turn-on to the Fish. Ms Leo feels sure that this rather mysterious character will blossom in her radiance, while Mr Leo longs to take care of the Mermaid. Trouble comes along when Leo inevitably bosses Pisces.

Pisces will put up with this for a while, but eventually glides away, becoming more and more evasive until he or she is just plain absent. Leo rants, raves, slips, and slides into red-faced perplexity, while Pisces feels sad – and absent again. For this to work, Pisces needs to be as up-front as possible and Leo needs to exercise all her or his imagination to understand what can never be really understood – the Piscean dreamscape.

As friends   You could find each other great fun. Leo will want to sort out Pisces' life and may get very frustrated when the Fish continues to wallow. Pisces must tell Leo not to be bossy, which won't prevent this happening but may moderate it, and Leo must learn that her or his sunny presence is enough – no answers are required.

As business partners   Bad news, unless you have some Earth in your charts. All too impractical – get some solid input from elsewhere.

Leo with Aries

Fierce, yet cheerful competition could be the order of the day. As two Fire signs you have much that is compatible between you. You may each find the other totally insufferable, but yet you gird up your loins and rejoin the fray – really you both enjoy it. It is unlikely that your relationship will ever become stale and cold.

As lovers   Passion runs high and expectations even higher. Both of you are great idealists and believe that love is, or should be, something larger than life and magical. With all the energy that you put into it, it probably will seem that way at first. Ms Leo is at her queenly best with the attentions of this dashing knight, while Mr Leo is enraptured by this exciting lady, who can answer all his own drive. Both of you have a great deal to give, and both are appreciative. After a while, however, Leo could feel insecure with Aries. You may both feel let down and unsure of what keeps you together. Always keep romance alive, do the unexpected, be that little bit special for each other and you will find the days of magic are not lost in the mists of time.

As friends You have lots in common. Yes, I am sure you will argue, but you will get on with things together and find much that fires you both. You are bound to compete and if you enjoy sport then so much the better, for you can compete physically. If not, there will be mental sparring. Make sure that plenty of shared activities divert your energies.

As business partners Lots of initiative but thin on the 'finishiative'. Both of you like getting things up and moving, but neither of you likes the boring details. Aries is full of 'I must do this, that or the other' and Leo, as the more constant of the two may be left to mop up, which makes a very angry Lion. You need an injection of practicality from elsewhere.

Leo with Taurus

You can both be very dogmatic. Leo is full of assurances while Taurus stubbornly goes his or her own way. This can result in impasse, and sometimes these two signs will refuse to speak to each other for days! However, in the end Leonine 'sunniness' and the more easy-going side of Taurus surface.

As lovers Earth and Fire again, and the sexual side may be extremely intense. Taurus is a very sensual sign and in many ways this is perfect for Leo – the ease with which Taurus relates to bodily matters reassures the Lion who feels confident of her or his own sexual expression. Ms Leo senses that this man can give her the stability that she needs and the opportunity to reign as the queen she is, while Mr Leo is devastated by the sex appeal of Ms Taurus. There is no reason why this relationship should not endure to Golden Anniversary as you both prize constancy. However, you will need to cultivate tolerance.

As friends You may hate each other on sight, as these signs are traditionally antipathetic. If the relationship gets going, however, there is much to recommend it. Leo can benefit from Taurean calmness, while Taurus appreciates Leo's cheery nature. You both enjoy gourmet delights and beautiful things of every description.

As business partners Well, this *should* work well, for you are the perfect complement to each other. Leo has the flair, the ideas, the drive, Taurus has the common sense and his or her own brand of creativity. The trouble is that Leo will get so frustrated and impatient at Taurean deliberation, and Taurus will simply dig in those Bull's hooves and kick up sand whenever Leonine Fire really starts to flare. The best thing is to apportion areas carefully and don't interfere in each other's sphere. Taurus must have the cheque book.

Leo with Gemini

You share a lively approach and a sense of fun. Leo finds the stimulating mind and quick tongue of Gemini fascinating. What may be less amusing is when Geminian mimicry dents the Lion's dignity. Nothing daunted, Gemini may continue with the repartee and the Lion is coaxed out of the sulks. You both love company and you may share a sense of humour. However, the Lion has strong emotional needs while those of Gemini are hard to define, so emotional rapport may be lacking.

As lovers Snap, crackle and pop at first. Leo finds Gemini endlessly intriguing and entertaining, aroused by the sheer breadth of

Geminian mental activity, while Gemini warms to Leo's zest. Ms Leo has respect for this Mr Gemini's quick mind and the way the '*bon mot*' trips so well from his tongue. Mr Leo responds to Ms Gemini's playfulness and skilful flirting. The champagne can go flat when Gemini feels caged by the Lion's demands and Leo feels plain insecure with Gemini. There is no more dangerous animal than a wounded Lion and sparks may fly. Nonetheless, there is so much mental compatibility here, that if you can compromise on emotional matters and talk fully about sexual ones – Leo's needs are the more intense – there is much to recommend this duo.

As friends   An excellent match. The two of you will have great fun together and do it in style. Any social event involving you can proceed with panache. If Leo hits a mournful patch Gemini will make her laugh, while Leonine constancy may be secretly reassuring to Gemini, without being boring.

As business partners   Enthusiasm and many ideas. Leo has the staying power to keep Gemini on track and isn't slow to spot the advantages of the Geminian input. Leo can assemble the large plan while Gemini is resourceful about the frills. Watch it – neither is good with money!

Leo with Cancer

The bonus here is that you both like taking care, and being cared for in different ways. Cancer can do a lot to make Leo feel secure, loved and very, very special. Leonine passion and breadth of vision can make Cancer feel like the Sun shines just for her or him – which it does. Happily the Crab basks. However, Leo may resent being fussed over too obviously, feeling that dignity is suffering. Sometimes Leo may blunder into treacherous waters and the Crab can withdraw for days, which is bad news. However, by giving all the loyalty the Lion needs, Cancer may succeed in softening Leo's approach so there can be much mutual tenderness.

As lovers Sex between you may be wonderful, and the emotional side is potentially fulfilling. Cancer responds with all the love that Leo dreams of, because Leo is a loyal, committed and very warm sign. Ms Leo may not be initially attracted to Mr Crab but becomes slowly fascinated by his depth, while Mr Leo responds to Cancerian sex appeal and becomes hooked. Long sulks may bedevil this relationship, however, and Leo gets supremely frustrated when Cancer cannot be induced to talk. It is very important here for Leo to develop sensitivity and patience, and for Cancer to try to be more frank about his or her feelings.

As friends Without the sexual side this could pose more problems, for Cancer may find Leo too assertive, and Leo may find Cancer a drag. However, you both respond to the good things in life. Leo secretly values the consolation of the Crab and Leo can often make Cancer laugh. Planned ventures that involve catering could be great, for the Crab's culinary expertise impresses Leo – and everyone.

As business partners Creative. Cancer has people skills, intuition and money sense. Leo has grandiose schemes and optimism.

Appendix 3

■ TRADITIONAL ASSOCIATIONS AND TOTEM

Each sign of the zodiac is said to have an affinity with certain colours, plants, stones and other substances. Of course, we cannot be definite about this, for not only do sources vary regarding specific correspondences – we also have the rest of the astrological chart to bear in mind. Some people also believe that the whole concept of such associations is invalid. However, there certainly do seem to be some links between the character of each of the signs and the properties of certain substances. It is up to you to experiment and to see what works for you.

Anything that traditionally links with Leo is liable to intensify Leonine traits. So if you wish for some reason to cultivate humility and a love for detail, then steer clear of the colour bright orange and frankincense essential oil! However, if you want to be your sunny Leonine best it may help to surround yourself with the right stimuli, especially on a down day. Here are some suggestions:

- **Colours**   Usually bright colours, especially shades of orange or gold. Anything dramatic.
- **Flowers**   Acacia, heliotrope, sunflower, orange blossom.
- **Metal**   Gold.
- **Stones**   Amber, carnelian, diamond, topaz.

Aromatherapy

Aromatherapy uses the healing power of essential oils both to prevent ill health and to maintain good health. Specific oils can sometimes be used to treat specific ailments. Essential oils are concentrated and powerful substances, and should be treated with respect. Buy from a reputable source. *Do not use any oil in pregnancy* until you have checked with a reputable source that it is okay (see 'Further Reading'). *Do not ingest oils* – they act through the subtle medium of smell, and are absorbed in massage. *Do not place undiluted on the skin.* For massage: Dilute in a carrier oil such as sweet almond or grapeseed, two drops of oil to one teaspoon of carrier. Use in an oil burner, six to ten drops at a time, to fragrance your living area.

Essential oils

- **Cinnamon** Warming and stimulating, good for combating fatigue. Antifungal. May irritate the skin, so use low concentration.
- **Frankincense** A rich and majestic oil. Helps relieve stress. Good for aiding meditation or concentration. Good also for respiratory problems.
- **Orange** Promotes energy and optimism. Combats digestive upsets, poor appetite and constipation. May irritate the skin, so use with care.
- **Sandalwood** Exotic and oriental, this is good for soothing throat problems. It is a sexual restorative and clears the mind of anxiety.
- **Rosemary** Sharp and warming, this is a heart tonic and stimulates the blood supply, especially to the brain. Helpful for combating aches and pains and lethargy.

Naturally, you are not restricted to oils ruled by your sign, for in many cases treatment by other oils will be beneficial, and you should consult a reputable source (see 'Further Reading') for advice if you have a particular problem. If a problem persists, consult your GP.

Your birth totem

According to the tradition of certain native North American tribes, each of the signs of the zodiac is known by a totem animal. The idea of the totem animal is useful, for animals are powerful, living symbols and they can do much to put us in touch with out potentials. Knowing your totem animal is different from knowing your sign, for your sign is used to define and describe you – as we have been doing in this book – whereas your totem shows you a path of potential learning and growth.

The totem for Leo is the Salmon, and you also have an affinity with Mouse and Hawk. You were born in the Ripening Time. There is a difficulty here, for the North American lore is based on the seasonal cycle. For those of you living in the Southern Hemisphere, it is worth bearing in mind the totems of your opposite sign, Aquarius. These are Otter, Buffalo and possibly Butterfly, though Butterfly links with Air. The Aquarian time is called Cleansing Time.

Salmon offers a slightly different perspective on Leo, for it is a fish and the fluid medium of water is its environment. It is a powerful, often very large fish, showing tremendous determination as it swims upstream to its breeding grounds. The Salmon appears frequently in Celtic myth, symbolising wisdom. Salmon may show Leo a gentler, intuitive, but no less regal way of being.

Contacting your totem

You can use visualisation techniques to make contact with the energies of your birth totem. You will need to be very quiet, still and relaxed. Make sure you won't be disturbed. Have a picture of your totem before you, and perhaps burn one of the oils we have mentioned, in an oil burner, to intensify the atmosphere. When you are ready close your eyes and imagine that you are your totem animal – imagine how it feels, what it sees, smells, tastes, hears. What are its feelings, instincts and abilities? Keep this up for as long as you are comfortable, then come back to everyday awareness. Write down your experiences and eat or drink something, to ground you. This can be a wonderfully refreshing and mind-clearing exercise, and you may find it inspiring. Naturally, if you feel you have other totem animals – creatures with which you feel an affinity – you are welcome to visualise those. Look out for your totems in the wild – there may be a message for you.

Further reading and resources

Astrology for Lovers, Liz Greene, Unwin, 1986. The title may be misleading, for this is a serious, yet entertaining and wickedly accurate account of the signs. A table is included to help you find your rising sign. This book is highly recommended.

Teach Yourself Astrology, Jeff Mayo and Christine Ramsdale, Hodder & Stoughton, 1996. A classic textbook for both beginner and practising astrologer, giving a fresh insight to birth charts through a unique system of personality interpretation.

Love Signs for Beginners, Kristyna Arcarti, Hodder & Stoughton, 1995. A practical introduction to the astrology of romantic relationships, explaining the different roles played by each of the planets and focussing particularly on the position of the Moon at the time of birth.

Star Signs for Beginners, Kristyna Arcarti, Hodder & Stoughton, 1993. An analysis of each of the star signs – a handy, quick reference.

The Moon and You for Beginners, Teresa Moorey, Hodder & Stoughton, 1996. Discover how the phase of the Moon when you were born affects your personality. This book looks at the nine lunar types – how they live, love, work and play, and provides simple tables to enable you to find out your birth phase and which type you are.

The New Compleat Astrologer, Derek and Julia Parker, Mitchell Beazley, 1984. This is a complete introduction to astrology with instructions on chart calculation and planetary tables, as well as clear and interesting descriptions of planets and signs. Including history and reviewing present-day astrology, this is an extensive work, in glossy, hardback form, with colour illustrations.

The Knot of Time: Astrology and the Female Experience, Lindsay River and Sally Gillespie. For personal growth, from a gently feminine perspective, this book has much wisdom.

The Astrology of Self-discovery, Tracy Marks, CRCS Publications, 1985. This book is especially useful for Moon signs.

The Astrologer's Handbook, Francis Sakoian and Louis Acker, Penguin, 1984. This book explains chart calculation and takes the reader through the meanings of signs and planets, with extensive interpretations of planets in signs and houses. In addition, all the major aspects between planets and angles are interpreted individually. A very useful work.

Aromatherapy for Pregnancy and Childbirth, Margaret Fawcett RGN, RM, LLSA, Element, 1993.

The Aromatherapy Handbook, Daniel Ryman, C W Daniel, 1990.

Useful addresses

The Faculty of Astrological Studies

The claim of the Faculty to provide the 'finest and most comprehensive astrological tuition in the world' is well founded. Correspondence courses of a high calibre are offered, leading to the internationally recognised diploma. Evening classes, seminars and summer schools are taught, catering for the complete beginner to the most experienced astrologer. A list of trained consultants can be supplied on request, if you wish for a chart interpretation. For further details telephone (UK code) 0171 700 3556 (24-hour answering service); or fax 0171 700 6479. Alternatively, you can write, with SAE, to: Ref. T. Moorey, FAS., BM7470, London WC1N 3XX, UK.

Educational

California Institute of Integral Studies, 765 Ashbury St, San Francisco, CA 94117. Tel: (415) 753-6100

Kepler College of Astrological Arts and Sciences, 4518 University Way, NE, Suite 213, Seattle, WA 98105. Tel: (206) 633-4907

Robin Armstrong School of Astrology, Box 5265, Station 'A', Toronto, Ontario, M5W 1N5, Canada. Tel: (416) 923-7827

Vancouver Astrology School, Astraea Astrology, Suite 412, 2150 W Broadway, Vancouver, V6K 4L9, Canada. Tel: (604) 536-3880

The Southern Cross Academy of Astrology, PO Box 781147, Sandton, SA 2146 (South Africa) Tel: 11-468-1157; Fax: 11-468-1522

Periodicals

American Astrology Magazine, PO Box 140713, Staten Island, NY 10314-0713. e-mail: am.astrology@genie.gies,com

The Journal of the Seasons, PO Box 5266, Wellesley St, Auckland 1, New Zealand. Tel/fax: (0)9-410-8416

The Federation of Australian Astrologers Bulletin, PO Box 159, Stepney, SA 5069. Tel/fax: 8-331-3057

Aspects, PO Box 2968, Rivonia 2128, SA (South Africa).
Tel: 11-864-1436

Realta, The Journal of the Irish Astrological Association, 4 Quay Street, Galway, Ireland. Available from IAA, 193, Lwr Rathmines Rd, Dublin 6, Ireland.

Astrological Association, 396 Caledonian Road, London, N1 1DN. Tel: (UK code) 0171 700 3746; Fax: 0171 700 6479. Bi-monthly journal issued.